complete

italian

complete
italian
cooking

Sonja Grey

First published in Great Britain in 1997 by
Hamlyn, a division of Octopus Publishing Group Limited
2–4 Heron Quays, London E14 4JP

This edition published in 2002

Distributed in the United States and Canada by
Sterling Publishing Co., Inc.
387 Park Avenue South, New York, NY 10016-8810

Printed in China

ISBN 0 600 60594 9

NOTES

Eggs should be medium to large unless otherwise stated.
The USDA advises that eggs should not be consumed raw. This
book contains dishes made with raw or lightly cooked eggs. It is
advisable for more vulnerable people such as pregnant and nursing
mothers, invalids, the elderly, babies, and young children to avoid
uncooked or lightly cooked dishes made with eggs. Once
prepared, these dishes should be kept refrigerated and used
quickly.

Meat and poultry should be cooked thoroughly. To test if poultry
is cooked, pierce the flesh through the thickest part with a skewer
or fork — the juices should run clear, never pink or red. Do not
re-freeze poultry that has been frozen previously and thawed.
Do not re-freeze a cooked dish that has been frozen previously.

Milk should be whole milk unless otherwise stated.

Nut and Nut Derivatives
This book includes dishes made with nuts and nut derivatives. It
is advisable for those with known allergic reactions to nuts and
nut derivatives and those who may be potentially vulnerable to
these allergies, such as pregnant and nursing mothers, invalids,
the elderly, babies, and children to avoid dishes made with nuts
and nut oils. It is also wise to check the labels of pre-prepared
ingredients for the possible inclusion of nut derivatives.

Pepper should be freshly ground black pepper unless otherwise
stated.

Fresh herbs should be used, unless otherwise stated. If
unavailable, use dried herbs as an alternative, but halve the
quantities stated.
Ovens should be pre-heated to the specified temperature — if
using a fan-assisted oven, follow the manufacturer's instructions
for adjusting the time and the temperature.

Vegetarians should ensure that cheeses are made with vegetarian
rennet. There are vegetarian forms of Parmesan, feta, Cheddar,
Cheshire, Monterey Jack, dolcelatte, goats' cheeses, and many
others.

Contents

Introduction

In Italy, good food and wine are a way of life — an intrinsic part of the Italian character and culture. Meals are important family rituals and consist of several courses. They often last for several hours.

According to its many enthusiastic and loyal devotees, Italian cuisine is second to none. People travel halfway across the continent of Europe not just to gaze at the many artistic splendors that Italy has to offer but also to enjoy the very special authentic home cooking that is on offer at every street corner.

There is plenty of choice available. On the one hand, there are small family tavernas and friendly little pizzerias, and on the other — at the opposite end of the economic scale — there are fancy restaurants that can serve you up a veritable banquet. Whatever you want to eat, and however much you have to spend, you are sure to find your heart's desire on a plate.

If you want to be sure of a good meal, follow your nose to the places where the locals eat, whether they be businessmen or truck-drivers. Do this, and you're likely to eat some of the best food in the world.

Variety is the spice of Italian cooking. There is something within the enormous Italian repertoire to suit every taste, every occasion, every age, and every pocket.

The history of Italian food

Italian cuisine has evolved over many centuries. It owes much to classic European traditions, including Roman, Byzantine and Greek.

Italian food as we know it today, however, derives from the Renaissance, and the many discoveries and inventions in the arts and sciences. One consequence of this exciting phase in European history was a new interest in food especially throughout northern and central Italy, in Florence, Milan and Rome. There was a sudden flowering of cookery skills, as the great rulers employed chefs who learned what to do with all the new ingredients that came from the Far East and the New World.

Classic recipes have been handed down over the years and through the generations. They are now an established part of family life throughout Italy.

Home cooking

The best cooking of all in Italy is found in the home. Italian women take enormous pleasure and pride in preparing wonderful dishes for their families — and this is something that you can do too.

Of course, you don't even have to travel to Italy to enjoy Italian food. Perhaps the most satisfying way of eating Italian food is to create some of their delicious dishes at home. It is not at all difficult, and your efforts will be well rewarded.

Italian cooking offers a wealth of delicious recipes— some straightforward and some satisfyingly complex, some simple, and some more ambitious, some modest, and some gloriously flamboyant.

Regional variations

Before Italy was united in 1870 by King Victor Emmanuel II, it was a collection of independent, neighboring states who frequently went to war with each other. As a result, the inhabitants of each state developed a tremendous pride of possession and a sense that everything their state did was better and more special than anywhere else. This applied to everything—their families, traditions, laws, customs, and, of course, food.

Even today, if you travel around Italy from one region to another, you will soon become aware not only of the differences in climate and landscape, but also of the differences in food. There is a wealth of different regional dishes, cheeses, and wines throughout Italy. For this reason, it has been said that to get to know Italy is to get to know the whole world of cookery.

The most noticeable difference is between northern and southern Italy. The north tends to be more industrial and more prosperous than the south, and the northern soil is also more fertile. The south is hotter and the landscape more arid.

As far as cooking is concerned, perhaps the most marked difference is in the different types of pasta. In the

north, it is flat, and freshly made with eggs. Tagliatelle, fettucine, and lasagne are particularly common in this part of Italy. In the south, on the other hand, tubular varieties of pasta, such as macaroni, spaghetti, ziti, bucatini, and rigatoni, are more common.

Arborio rice is grown in the north, in the Po Valley just beyond Venice, where it is eaten as a staple ingredient, alongside pasta. Arborio rice is a particularly absorbent type of medium-grain rice and is used to make risottos, such as the classic Milanese risotto.

In the north, the fat used for cooking is generally butter. In the south, it is olive oil. In the north, delicious cakes and pastries are often eaten, and display a distinctly Teutonic influence, as does the popularity of game. In the south, the flavors are much stronger, due to generous use of herbs and spices, especially in the sauces.

The one thing that all the regions of Italy have in common is their joyful approach to food and cooking. There is nothing solemn or self-righteous about food here. Eating is rather one long light-hearted variation on a well-loved theme.

A healthy way

Italian food is not only delicious, it is also one of the healthiest ways of eating in the world. There is no mystery about why this is the case—a quick look at all the staple ingredients soon provides the answer.

Olive oil, fresh vegetables, salads, fresh fish, seafood, pasta, rice: these are all mouthwatering foods, but they are also very healthy. Full of vitamins and minerals, they are also extremely low in saturated fat.

It is no surprise, then, that Italian cooking is particularly beneficial to a healthy heart. It is also no coincidence that the Italians have such a low incidence of heart disease.

The Italian way of eating, now acknowledged to be one of the healthiest in the world, clearly pays rich dividends. It therefore makes good sense to incorporate these ingredients into your day-to-day cooking.

Ingredients

The Italians are fortunate in having such a cornucopia of marvelous ingredients at their disposal. Italian women love to go out shopping in the colorful street markets and grocery stores where they regularly stock up on all their preferred ingredients. With these on hand they are always ready to make their favorite — and their family's favorite — dishes.

Perhaps most important of all, the Italians treat their ingredients with great respect. There are no random choices in the way they shop or cook. They select their ingredients carefully, they store them wisely, and they use them judiciously.

Essential pantry ingredients for cooking the Italian way are simple. The most important ingredient of all is probably olive oil. It's best to invest in a light one for cooking and a heavier, fuller-flavored one for making salads. Details of typical ingredients are given in special features throughout this book.

Pantry essentials

If you want to cook Italian dishes, it is useful to keep a store of the following non-perishable items in your pantry, as they will all come in useful.
• Pasta is perhaps what people think of first when they think of Italian food. It is available both fresh and dried.

Many people prefer the fresh kind, but even if this applies to you a stock of dried pasta is essential to cope with all emergencies. Pasta is made with durum wheat flour bound with eggs, oil, or both. Sometimes it is colored with spinach or beets. It is a good idea to keep a range of different pastas in the cupboard, including a few of the less common shapes. The small varieties are useful for adding to soups.
• Rice is the other main staple food in Italy, along with pasta. Italian Arborio rice is a short, round-grained rice, which absorbs more liquid than other types of rice and is particularly good for making creamy risottos.
• Canned tomatoes are an absolute must in Italian cooking. Canned plum tomatoes are full of flavor, as well as being an excellent, inexpensive convenience food. They are also sold ready-chopped, and even flavored with garlic or herbs.
• Tomato paste adds flavor and color to any dish in which fresh or canned tomatoes are used.
• Olives are frequently used in Italian cooking. As well as being useful ingredients in antipasti, they are also included in sauces and casserole dishes. Keep a stock of green, black, and stuffed olives in bottles, and buy fresh loose ones whenever possible, as these are the best.
• Capers are another excellent standby, which add flavor and authenticity to various fish dishes. They also add zest to certain sauces, as well as being a useful garnish.
• Antipasti are available in jars from many supermarkets and are a useful standby for including in many dishes. They include sun-dried tomatoes (delicious chopped up and used in pasta sauces), artichoke hearts, wild mushrooms, and marinated peppers.
• Pesto, made with basil, Parmesan cheese, and olive oil, is best made fresh, but the varieties available in jars are a very acceptable alternative. Red pesto has sun-dried tomatoes added to it. You can use it on pasta, or incorporate it into a pasta sauce.

Constructing a menu

The Italian style of eating is to start with an *antipasto*, such as stuffed vegetables, salami or other dried sausage, or seafood salad. A soup, or *minestra*, or a pasta usually follows, rarely both. Sometimes there is also a vegetable course. The *piatto di mezzo* follows. This means "the middle dish", or entrée, and usually consists of meat, poultry, or fish, often accompanied by a salad, or, more rarely, a cooked vegetable.

Finally, there is the dessert. Desserts are very important in Italy. They may consist of nothing more complicated than fresh fruit in season, but they may consist of a delicious ice cream—no one makes ice creams better than the Italians — or there may be an elaborate dessert or cake.

Either way, the dessert is usually the finishing touch; cheese is rarely served at the end of a meal, but is more frequently part of the antipasto, or eaten as a snack at some other time of day.

Meals are always a great social event in Italy. The occasion brings everyone together, from the youngest member of the family to the oldest.

Lunch is probably the most important meal of the day, and people devote two hours to it. Factories and stores close and everyone rushes home or, if they live too far away, they make their way to a favorite restaurant. The midday meal consists of several courses, each of which has equal importance.

Pasta

Devotees are convinced that fresh pasta is far superior to the dried kind. Fortunately, fresh pasta is easy to make at home, with or without a pasta machine. A machine is simple to use and will give you a more uniform result, but it is perfectly possible to make excellent pasta dough without a machine and to cut the dough by hand. Whatever method you use, it is well worth the effort, because the end result will be greatly superior to the dried, manufactured product. Failing that, though, fresh pasta is easily available from Italian delis, specialist Italian shops, and supermarkets.

Pizza

Mention Italian food and most people think immediately of pizzas. Pizza can be served as a one-course meal, or can stave off hunger in the form of a quick and easy snack.

Naples is reputed to be the original home of the pizza, and is considered to be the culinary center of the south. Pizzas are now found all over Italy and are baked in open brick, wood-fired ovens in pizzerias and bakeries.

Wine

Italy is the largest wine producer in the world. It is also high in the world's drinking league, with some 120 bottles being consumed per person per year.

Many Italian wines are imported but a good, Italian-style California wine can be substituted. Each region of Italy produces its own wine. Barolo is made in Piedmont; this robust red wine goes well with roasts and game. So does another local wine, Barbera, perfect fare for drinking with pasta and pizzas. Veneto produces Valpolicella and Soave, while Tuscany is home to the great Chianti Classico. Chianti is also an excellent wine to drink with roasted, broiled, and barbecued meats. Fortified wines, such as dry white vermouth and marsala, are stronger

than table wines and are a delicious addition to a dish, to which they will impart an excellent flavor.

Fresh stock recipes

You will find it very useful to refer to these basic recipes as they are required throughout this book.

A well-flavored stock is easy, satisfying, and inexpensive to make, and uses only a few basic ingredients. It is really not necessary to resort to stock cubes, when the flavor of a deliciously fresh, aromatic, broth is far superior. If you are making beef or fish stock, you should be able to find the bones you need in the market. Once made, stock can be chilled, then frozen. Freeze stock in small batches in plastic tubs or ice trays. When frozen, the cubes can be transferred to clearly labeled plastic bags for ease of storage.

Every cook needs to know the few basic rules for making a good stock. If you follow them, you will find that your finished dishes will taste much better. You will never want to use a cube again!
• Stock should always simmer extremely gently, or it will evaporate too quickly and become cloudy.
• never add salt to the stock. Simmering reduces the liquid and concentrates the flavor. This will affect the flavor of the finished dish. Salt should only be added to the dish in which the stock is being used .
• Any scum that rises to the surface should be removed as it appears, otherwise it will spoil the color and flavor of the finished stock.
• Avoid root vegetables with a floury texture as these will cause the stock to become cloudy.

Beef stock
• Put 5 pounds beef, or beef and veal, bones in a roasting pan, and place in a preheated 450° F oven. Roast for 1 hour or until browned and the fat and juices run out. Using a slotted spoon, transfer the bones to a large pot.
• Place the roasting pan on top of the stove, add 2 roughly chopped onions, 2 roughly chopped carrots, and 2 roughly chopped celery stalks. Fry gently in the remaining fat until nicely browned, but do not burn. Add the vegetables to the bones in the saucepan, together with 2 bay leaves, a few parsley stalks, 2 sprigs thyme, 10 whole peppercorns, and cover with 5 quarts cold water.
• Bring to the boil, skimming any scum from the surface. Reduce the heat to very low and simmer, uncovered, for 8 hours, skimming occasionally. Strain the stock and cool it then refrigerate it. Remove any fat on the surface by skimming lightly with a paper towel. Once the stock is completely cold it can be frozen.

Makes about 2¾ quarts
Preparation time: 5–10 minutes
Cooking time: about 9 hours

"The one thing that all the regions of Italy have in common is their joyful approach to food and cooking."

Chicken stock
• Chop a cooked chicken carcass into 3 or 4 pieces and place it in a large pot with neck and gizzard, and the trimmings, 1 roughly chopped onion, 2 roughly chopped large carrots, and 1 roughly chopped celery stalk, 1 bay leaf, a few lightly crushed parsley stalks, and 1 sprig thyme, and cover with 1¾ quarts cold water.
• Bring to the boil, removing any scum from the surface. Reduce the heat and simmer for 2–2½ hours. Strain the stock through a muslin-lined sieve and leave to cool.

Makes 1 quart
Preparation time: 5–10 minutes
Cooking time: about 2½ hours

Fish stock
Do not use the bones of oily fish, such as tuna and mackerel, for fish broth. It is also very important that the stock does not boil

• In a large pot, place 3 pounds fish trimmings and 1 onion, sliced, the white part of a small leek, 1 celery stalk, 1 bay leaf, 6 parsley stalks, 10 whole peppercorns, and 1 pint dry white wine into a large pot, and cover with 1¾ quarts cold water.

• Bring slowly to just below boiling point. Simmer for 20 minutes, removing any scum from the surface. Line a sieve with cheesecloth and strain the stock through it. Leave to cool completely before refrigerating.

Makes 1¾ quarts
Preparation time: 10 minutes
Cooking time: 20 minutes

Vegetable stock
This recipe for vegetable stock can be varied to your own taste, and adapted according to what vegetables you have available. For example, you can try adding some fennel bulb for a mild aniseed flavor, or a sliver of orange zest for an added lift. The addition of tomatoes will give the finished stock extra richness of flavor and color. Remember to avoid using any floury root vegetables as these will cause the stock to become cloudy.
• In a deep pot, place 1 pound chopped mixed vegetables such as, carrots, leeks, celery, onion, and mushrooms, in equal quantities. Add 1 clove garlic, 6 peppercorns, 1 bouquet garni (2 parsley sprigs, 2 sprigs thyme, and 1 bay leaf) in a pan, and cover with 3 pints water.
• Bring to the boil and simmer gently, uncovered, for 30 minutes, skimming off any scum when necessary. Strain, and cool the stock completely before refrigerating.

Makes 1 quart
Preparation time: 5–10 minutes
Cooking time: about 45 minutes

Cook's tools

"It is not really an exaggeration to say that peace and happiness begin, geographically, where garlic is used in cooking."

Marcel Boulestin

The gentle art of cooking is not for the faint-hearted. But if the cook can stand the heat in the kitchen, so must the tools he or she chooses and uses. Safe in the dishwasher, smooth, stainless steel saucepans, cool, marble chopping blocks, sharp, cooks' knives, blenders, and whisks all form part of the "batterie de cuisine" of any chef worth his or her salt. Here are some basic guidelines, but the golden rule is to buy the best quality utensils you can afford!

Colander

Colanders are used for separating liquids and solids, and for draining and rinsing foods. They come in many different shapes and sizes, but a colander is basically a container with holes in it. It is usually made of metal or plastic. Buy a colander which is big enough to hold the vegetables but not too large to rest in your sink.

Pizza/Pasta cutter

As the name suggests this is a useful implement for cutting pizzas, pastry, or pasta. When choosing a cutter, ensure that the wheel turns freely and that there is a guard to protect your fingers. The wheel should be stainless steel and the handle should be made from wood, metal, or plastic.

Grater

Graters come in both a box shape or a single flat sheet. Both shapes have perforations which perform different functions. The fine holes are for grating spices and rind, the medium and large holes are for grating cheese and vegetables. Graters are generally made of stainless steel, as it is hard-wearing and does not rust. Special Parmesan graters are available too. These have a drawer underneath to catch the finely grated hard cheese. If you have a flat sheet grater, ensure that it is properly balanced when grating, as this type has a tendency to slip.

Measuring cup

A measuring cup is a standardized measure of liquid. It has a handle and a good pouring lip. It is often marked in both American and metric measures, fractions of pints, and fluid ounces as well as milliliters and liters. Cups are available in glass, plastic, or stainless steel. However, it is advisable to check before purchasing a cup that it is dishwasher safe.

Pasta server

A pasta server is a large stainless steel or plastic spoon with a long handle, used for transferring pasta or noodles from the pan to the serving dish. It has characteristic "teeth" which pick up spaghetti and tagliatelle easily and a hole which lets liquid drain away.

Pizza Brick or Stone

This is used to bake pizza or flat bread instead of a baking tray. It is not essential but it is very useful for authentic, even, cooking. It is made of terracotta brick as this retains the heat well and also crisps the bottom of the pizza during baking.

Garlic Press

A garlic press is used to finely crush garlic cloves by forcing the flesh through holes. This releases the oils and the full flavor of the garlic into the dish. This useful tool also saves the pungent aroma of garlic lingering on the skin, as it avoids the need to handle the juices from the crushed garlic.

Pizza Spatula

A pizza spatula is a wide-bladed slice used to lift and transfer the pizza from the baking tray to the serving dish. It is generally made of stainless steel.

Metal Spatula

A metal spatula is a flexible, round-bladed knife with no sharp edges. It is used for smoothing or scraping and is very handy in baking. The best spatulas are made of stainless steel, but they are also available in rigid plastic.

Special utensils

Pasta machine

Rolling pin

Pasta machine

If you make pasta regularly it is worth investing in a pasta machine which will ease the making of noodles and pasta considerably. The dough mixture is fed into the machine through the rollers until it comes out in a smooth elastic sheet. This process may have to be repeated several times. It is possible to buy attachments for a basic machine which will cut the flat sheet of dough into ribbons of tagliatelle, and other pasta widths.

Rolling pin

A rolling pin is used for rolling out pasta and bread dough or pastry, into a smooth, flat, even sheet. A rolling pin can be made of wood, plastic, nylon, or marble and should be wide, heavy and well balanced.

When rolling out a dough or pastry mixture, sprinkle the rolling pin with a little flour to stop the mixture sticking to the pin. After use, remember to wipe the rolling pin thoroughly to ensure that it is clean prior to being stored.

Ravioli pan

Olive oil canister

Ravioli mold

Ravioli pan

A ravioli pan is a metal tray mold with indentations to make the ravioli shapes. A small rolling pin is usually provided in order to push out the ravioli.

Ravioli mold

A ravioli mold is a single mold used to press out two shapes of ravioli from the pasta sheet. The pasta is then filled with the chosen stuffing.

Olive oil canister

This canister has a particularly long, thin spout which is useful for distributing oil evenly over salads, pans, and utensils. It ensures that there is no unnecessary wastage. It is best to invest in a small canister to use while you are cooking, but you should not store oil in this way, as it spoils the oil and

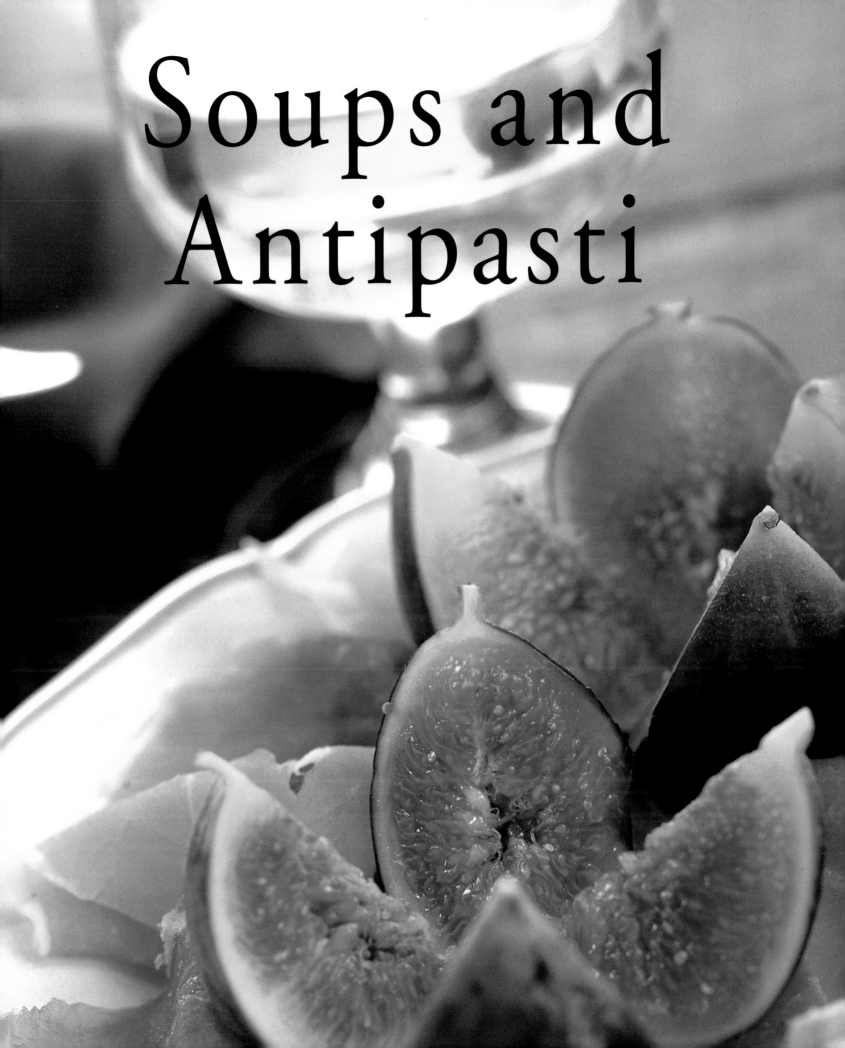

Soups and Antipasti

Zucchini Soup
with Parmesan crostini

This is a fresh, light-textured soup with a delicate flavor. It can be made any time of year, since zucchini are always in season.

3 tablespoons butter
I onion, sliced
4 cups thinly sliced zucchini,
I quart Chicken Broth (see page 11)
2 small eggs
2 tablespoons grated Parmesan cheese
I tablespoon chopped basil or parsley
salt and pepper
crostini or croûtons, to garnish

melt the butter in a saucepan, add the onion, and fry gently for 5 minutes. Add the zucchini and fry, stirring frequently for 5–10 minutes. Add the chicken broth, bring to a boil, cover, and simmer for 20 minutes.

purée in an electric blender or rub through a sieve. Return to the saucepan and bring to a boil.

beat together the eggs, cheese, and herbs in a warmed soup tureen, then slowly beat in the boiling soup. Check the seasoning and pour into individual soup bowls.

garnish with crostini or croûtons and serve immediately.

Serves 4–6
Preparation time: *25–30 minutes*
Cooking time: *20 minutes*

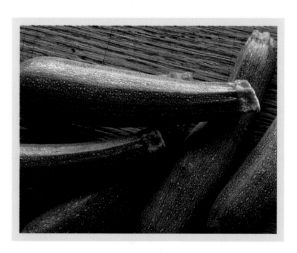

clipboard: To make crostini, cut kaiser rolls into slices ¼ inch thick and toast one side. Spread the untoasted side with butter, sprinkle thickly with grated cheese, and place under a preheated hot broiler until golden and bubbling.

Country-style Minestrone

This is one of the best known Italian soups, a hearty, warming, peasant dish, substantial enough to provide a whole meal in itself.

½ cup cannellini beans
3 tablespoons oil
2 onions, chopped
2 garlic cloves, crushed
2–3 rindless bacon slices, chopped
1¾ quarts water
1 teaspoon chopped fresh marjoram
½ teaspoon chopped fresh thyme
4 tomatoes, skinned (see clipboard below), seeded, and chopped
2 carrots, diced
2 potatoes, diced
1 small turnip, diced
1–2 celery sticks
2 cups shredded cabbage
½ cup small pasta shapes
3 tablespoons grated Parmesan cheese, plus extra to serve
salt and freshly ground pepper

To garnish
1 teaspoon chopped fresh parsley
sprig fresh thyme, to garnish

place the cannellini beans in a large bowl and cover with water. Leave them to soak for 8 hours or overnight. Drain the beans and then rinse under running cold water.

heat the oil in a large saucepan and add the onions, garlic and bacon. Sauté gently for about 5 minutes, stirring occasionally, until the onions are soft and golden brown.

add the beans, water, herbs and tomatoes, cover the pan and simmer gently for 2 hours. Add the carrots and simmer for 10 minutes. Stir in the potatoes and turnip and cook for another 10 minutes.

chop the celery and shred the cabbage. Add to the soup with the pasta shapes and cook for 10 minutes, or until the pasta and all the vegetables are tender. Season to taste. Stir in the Parmesan and then ladle into individual soup bowls. Serve immediately, sprinkled with extra Parmesan and garnish with fresh parsley and thyme.

Serves 6
Preparation time: *20 minutes, plus soaking overnight*
Cooking time: *2½ hours*

clipboard: to skin tomatoes, place them in a bowl and pour enough boiling water over them to cover. Leave for 1–2 minutes, then drain, cut a cross at the stem end of each tomato, and peel off the skins.

Smoked Ham and Bean Soup
scented with garlic

1 ½ cups dried pinto or cannellini beans
1 carrot, chopped
1 onion, quartered
1 bouquet garni
½ cup cooked smoked ham, cubed
2 shallots, finely chopped
1 garlic clove, crushed
3 tablespoons butter
1 tablespoon chopped parsley
salt and freshly ground black pepper
½ tablespoon chopped parsley, to garnish
½ cup croûtons, to serve

soak the beans overnight in cold water, drain. Bring the beans to the boil over a medium heat in a large pan with 2 quarts lightly salted water. Add the carrot, onion, bouquet garni, and ham. Leave to simmer for 2 hours, or until the beans are tender.

pour the soup in a blender or food processor, first removing the bouquet garni. Return the purée to the pan and reheat over a medium heat.

cook the shallots and garlic in the butter in a heavy pan. When they have turned color, add the chopped parsley and mix quickly. Turn off the heat and add this mixture to the bean purée.

mix well with a wooden spoon, add a good sprinkling of pepper and the extra parsley, then pour into individual bowls. Serve the croûtons separately.

Serves 4
Preparation time: *30 minutes, plus overnight soaking*
Cooking time: *2 hours*

Salamis
and sausage l...

Parma Ham

Pancetta

Fresh Italian Sausage

Mortadello

Parma Ham
Parma ham (or Prosciutto) comes from Parma. Because of its long curing process the ham commands a high price. Parma ham is pink in color and marbled with white fat. It is sliced wafer thin and is often served with melon or figs as an antipasto.

Pancetta
Pancetta is unsmoked bacon taken from the belly of a pig. It is cured with spices, salt and pepper. The bacon is then rolled into a sausage shape and sliced very thinly. Pancetta is also very popular diced and fried with garlic and onions.

Fresh Italian Sausage
Italian fresh sausages are made in various shapes and sizes and spiced with garlic, pepper, fennel and wine. Salamelle and Zampone are typical examples. They are traditionally poached whole and are served hot with potato salad or vegetables.

Mortadello
Mortadello is a large, slightly smoked sausage made from pure pork or a mixture of meats. It is seasoned with parsley and studded with olives and pistachio nuts. It is thinly sliced or diced and eaten cold in sandwiches or salads.

ks

Spinata Romana

Bresaola

Bocconcino

Ferrara Salami

Bocconcino
Bocconcino are small, sausage-shaped salamis sold in a string. They are made of raw pork or other red meat, interspersed with fat, and are highly seasoned. Bocconcino should be sliced very finely and used in salads and sandwiches.

Bresaola
Bresaola is a high quality salted, raw beef which is very expensive as it goes through a long, complicated curing process. It is served in very thin slices as an antipasto and is delicious with a simple dressing of olive oil, lemon juice, and pepper.

Ferrara Salami
Ferrara salami is one of the countless varieties of regional Italian salamis. It is a large salami made of raw meat which has been seasoned with garlic and pepper. It is served sliced as an antipasto and is also good in sandwiches and as an addition to salads.

Spinata Romana
Spinata Romana is a speciality of the countryside around Rome. It is a large square-shaped salami with a distinctive appearance, papery texture, and a mild taste. It is studded through with large chunks of pork fat and peppercorns.

White Bean
and vermicelli soup

A nourishing, country-style soup to serve on cold winter evenings.

1 cup canellini, navy or Great Northern beans, soaked overnight

8 ounces pork belly with skin

1 onion, finely chopped

1 carrot, finely chopped

1 celery stick, finely chopped

1 garlic clove, crushed

3 parsley sprigs, finely chopped

1 sprig of sage, chopped

1 bay leaf

6 ounces vermicelli, spaghetti, or ribbon noodles

2 tablespoons olive oil

salt and freshly ground black pepper

drain the beans and put in a large saucepan with the pork, onion, carrot, celery, garlic, parsley, sage, bay leaf, and enough water to cover. Bring to a boil, then reduce the heat, cover the pan, and simmer gently for 2 hours, or until the beans are soft.

grind one cupful of beans in a food mill or rub through a sieve. Stir the puréed beans back into the soup. Season to taste with salt and pepper, and bring back to the boil.

add the vermicelli, spaghetti, or noodles, and boil about 12 minutes, or until the pasta is cooked and tender, but still firm to the bite (*al dente*).

remove the pork from the soup. Cut off the rind and cut the meat into small pieces. Just before serving, drizzle the olive oil into the soup, stir in the pork, and a generous grinding of black pepper. Transfer to a tureen or individual serving dishes.

Serves 4–6
Preparation time: *20 minutes plus soaking overnight*
Cooking time: *2½ hours*

clipboard: This is one of many versions of soups which can be made with different kinds of dried beans combined with pasta or noodles. These soups are usually described as *pasta con fagioli* or *pasta e fagioli*.

Garlic Crostini
with chicken liver pâté

These crunchy tidbits are special enough to prepare as a light snack in themselves, as well as being a delicious appetizer for a dinner party.

¼ cup butter

I small onion, finely chopped

I–2 garlic cloves, crushed

I cup chicken livers, trimmed of all sinew

2 anchovy fillets

I tablespoon cream

2–3 tablespoons Marsala

pinch of paprika

½ inch slices of bread cut diagonally from a small French loaf

olive oil for frying

2–3 extra garlic cloves, halved

salt and pepper

I tablespoon chopped parsley, to serve

small amount of paprika to garnish (optional)

heat the butter in a skillet and cook the onion and garlic until soft but not colored. Add the chicken livers and cook gently for about 10 minutes until they just turn color, then add the anchovy fillets.

purée the liver mixture in a food processor or blender until smooth. Add the cream and sufficient Marsala to give a soft, spreadable consistency. Add the paprika and season to taste. Keep hot.

fry the slices of bread in hot olive oil until golden brown on both sides. Rub the garlic over one surface of each slice of bread and cover with the liver pâté.

sprinkle a little chopped parsley and a little paprika, if desired, over each slice just before serving. Serve hot.

Serves 4
Preparation time: *20 minutes*
Cooking time: *20–30 minutes*

clipboard: Instead of frying the bread, rub the garlic over each slice of bread, then dip the bread into olive oil and place on a baking tray. Bake in a preheated hot oven at 450°F for 12–15 minutes or until golden brown. Turn once or twice during baking so that the bread colors evenly on both sides.

Vegetable Antipasto
with bell peppers and leeks

This is a wonderfully tasty appetizer, combining the smoky taste of broiled peppers and pungent leeks. Broiled vegetables are very much in keeping with new trends in healthy eating.

For the pepper salad

4 red, green, and yellow bell peppers

4 tablespoons olive oil

1 tablespoon chopped, fresh parsley

2 garlic cloves, crushed or chopped

freshly ground sea salt

For the leeks in vinaigrette

1 pound thin leeks, washed and trimmed

6 tablespoons olive oil

1 tablespoon lemon juice

2 tablespoons balsamic or wine vinegar

2 garlic cloves, crushed

sea salt and freshly ground black pepper

place the peppers under a hot broiler and cook until they are black and blistered. Turn them occasionally to cook them evenly on all sides. Place in a plastic bag until they are cool, and then peel away the skins.

cut the peppers open and remove all the seeds. Cut the flesh into thin strips and arrange them on a serving dish, Sprinkle with olive oil and scatter with parsley and garlic. Finally, sprinkle a little sea salt over the peppers.

cook the leeks in a large saucepan of lightly salted boiling water for about 10 minutes or until they are tender but still firm. Drain them thoroughly in a colander, and transfer them to a serving dish.

make the vinaigrette: mix together the olive oil, lemon juice, vinegar, garlic, and seasoning until well blended. Pour the dressing over the leeks and serve either warm or cold with the pepper salad and some fresh ciabatta or crusty bread.

Serves 4–6
Preparation time: *30 minutes*
Cooking time: *15 minutes*

Parma Ham
with figs or melon

Parma Ham or Prosciutto is considered a great delicacy in Italy in the same way as Smithfield ham is in the U.S. It combines beautifully with fresh figs or melon for a great summer appetizer.

8 ripe purple figs
4 slices Parma ham or raw smoked ham (if available)
freshly ground black pepper, to season

Variation
1 sweet ripe melon, chilled
4 slices Parma ham, or raw smoked ham (if available)
freshly ground black pepper, to serve

cut the figs almost through into quarters.

arrange the ham on individual plates and top with the figs. Serve with freshly ground black pepper.

Variation
cut the melon into quarters and remove the seeds.

drape the slices of ham over the melon. Serve with freshly ground black pepper.

Serves 4
Preparation time: *10 minutes*

clipboard: This is the easiest of all *antipasti* to prepare, yet, because of its simplicity, the ingredients must be of the finest quality. Experiment with different kinds of melons, such as Crenshaw or Honeydew. Raw ham may not be available commercially in some states; always use the best quality country ham, sliced paper-thin.

Onion Savory

on Italian bread

Some of the traditional Italian breads such as ciabatta and focaccia are made with olive oil, and these make the perfect base for this aromatic savory dish. You can also serve it as a tasty snack with soup.

1½ pounds onions, sliced
2 tablespoons olive oil
½ cup chopped bacon
a few basil leaves, torn
3 medium tomatoes, skinned (see page 20) and mashed
3 eggs, beaten
¾ cup Parmesan cheese, grated
4 slices of hot toasted ciabatta or focaccia (or other bread made with olive oil)
salt and pepper
extra basil leaves, shredded, to garnish

put the onions in a bowl, cover with cold water, and soak overnight.

heat the oil in a large, heavy-based skillet with a lid. Add the bacon, and fry gently until browned. Drain the onions thoroughly, then add to the pan with the basil, and salt and pepper to taste. Cook over low heat for 20 minutes, stirring occasionally.

add the tomatoes, cover the skillet, lower the heat, and cook very gently for 10 minutes. Taste and adjust the seasoning. Beat the eggs and Parmesan together, then add to the pan. Remove from the heat immediately and stir vigorously.

put a slice of hot toast in each individual soup bowl, then spoon the hot savory over each slice. Serve immediately, garnished with the basil.

Serves 4
Preparation time: *20 minutes, plus overnight soaking*
Cooking time: *30 minutes*

clipboard: You can make your own olive oil bread easily if you prefer (see pages 248-250.) This savory dish is a good way of using up bread that is a couple of days old.

Fish and Shellfish

Fresh Sardines
with pine nuts and anchovies

6 tablespoons olive oil

2 cups fresh white bread crumbs

3 tablespoons golden raisins, soaked in hot water and drained

3 tablespoons pine nuts (pignolas)

1 tablespoon chopped parsley

1 x 1½ ounce can anchovies, drained and chopped

pinch of nutmeg

1½ pounds sardines, heads and backbones removed

approximately 12 bay leaves

4 tablespoons lemon juice

salt and pepper

To garnish

lemon wedges

heat 4–5 tablespoons of oil in a skillet and fry half the bread crumbs over moderate heat, turning them frequently with a metal spatula until they are a light golden brown.

remove from the heat and add the raisins, pine nuts, parsley, anchovies, and nutmeg. Season to taste with salt and pepper.

place a little of the mixture inside each sardine and press the sides together to close. Arrange rows of sardines in a single layer in a large oiled oven-to-table dish. Place half a bay leaf between each sardine.

sprinkle the remaining breadcrumbs and the oil over the top and bake in a preheated oven at 350°F for 30 minutes. Sprinkle the lemon juice over the top just before serving. Serve hot, garnished with lemon wedges.

Serves 4
Preparation time: *30–35 minutes*
Cooking time: *40–50 minutes*
Oven temperature: 350°F

clipboard: If fresh sardines are not available, other small fresh oily fish, such as small shad or mackerel, can be used instead.

Baby Squid
with spinach and tomatoes

2–3 tablespoons olive oil

1 onion, chopped

1–2 garlic cloves, crushed

1 fresh chili pepper, chopped

1 stick celery, chopped

2 tablespoons chopped parsley, plus extra to garnish

1¼ pounds baby squid (calamari), cleaned and cut into ½ inch slices

2 teaspoons plain flour

1 cup mushrooms, quartered or thickly sliced

3 large tomatoes, peeled, seeded and chopped

4 cups fresh chopped spinach

1¼ cups dry white wine

salt and pepper

heat the oil in a large pan, and add the onions, garlic, chili pepper, and celery, and cook gently until the onion is golden brown,

add the parsley and squid, and cook gently for an additional 10 minutes. Stir in the flour, mix well and then add the mushrooms, tomatoes, spinach, and white wine. Season to taste with salt and pepper.

cover and simmer very gently for about 30 minutes or until the squid is nearly cooked, then remove the lid and simmer until the sauce thickens and the squid is completely tender.

check the seasoning and pour into a hot serving dish. Serve hot, garnished with the extra chopped parsley.

Serves 4
Preparation time: *30–35 minutes*
Cooking time: *50–55 minutes*

clipboard: Squid (calamari) must be cooked very gently if it is not to become rubbery. Length of cooking time will depend on size. For the best results with this dish, choose baby squid.

Saffron Fish
with sweet peppers and tomatoes

This is a delicious way of cooking firm, white-fleshed fish such as cod or red snapper. It makes an aromatic dish.

½ teaspoon saffron strands
1¼ pounds cod fillet or other firm white fish
1 tablespoon flour
3 tablespoons oil
2 yellow bell peppers, seeded and cut into strips
2 tomatoes, chopped
1 small onion, finely chopped
1 garlic clove, finely chopped
1 tablespoon chopped parsley
salt and pepper
slices of polenta, to serve (optional)

put the saffron strands to soak in a little hot water.

cut the fish fillets into even-sized pieces and dust with flour. Heat the oil in a large shallow skillet, add the fish, and cook over medium heat for a few minutes, turning once until golden.

season with salt and pepper, remove with a spatula and keep warm.

add the prepared vegetables to the pan and cook, stirring until golden. Season with a pinch of salt, reduce the heat, cover with a lid and simmer for about 30 minutes.

stir in the saffron liquid halfway though.

when the vegetables are almost cooked, add the pieces of cod and sprinkle with chopped parsley. Serve hot with slices of polenta, if desired.

Serves 4
Preparation time: *10 minutes*
Cooking time: *35 minutes*

clipboard: Polenta is warming and filling, and is Italian equivalent of mashed potatoes. It is the Italian version of cornmeal mush and is eaten sliced, sometimes cold.

Fresh Tuna
with anchovies and mushrooms

Tuna is very popular in Italy, and appears in many traditional dishes. This recipe is simple, elegant, and gratifyingly easy to prepare.

4–6 tablespoons oil
2–3 garlic cloves, crushed
1 large onion, finely chopped
1¼ cups button mushrooms, quartered or thickly sliced
6–8 anchovy fillets, chopped
2 tablespoons chopped parsley
1 tablespoon all-purpose flour
1¼ cups dry white wine
pepper
pinch of nutmeg
4 x 6–8 ounce tuna steaks, about ½ inch thick

heat the oil in a skillet and cook the garlic and onion until soft and lightly colored. Add the mushrooms and cook for 2–3 minutes, then add the anchovies, parsley, and flour. Mix together well.

stir in the wine, bring to a boil, stirring all the time, then simmer gently for 5–7 minutes.

season to taste with pepper and a pinch of nutmeg. There should be no need to add salt because the anchovies are salty.

place the tuna steaks in an oven-to-table dish and pour over the sauce.

cover with a lid or aluminum foil and cook in a preheated oven at 375°F for 40–45 minutes. Serve hot.

Serves 4
Preparation time: *15–20 minutes*
Cooking time: *55–60 minutes*
Oven temperature: *375°F*

clipboard: Swordfish or shark steaks could equally well be used in this recipe, in place of tuna.

Fish Steaks
with tomato and garlic sauce

4 x 5 ounce white fish steaks, such as sea bass,
redfish or red snapper
3 tablespoons olive oil

Marinade
5 tablespoons olive oil
juice of ½ lemon
1 tablespoon finely chopped fresh parsley

Tomato sauce
2 tablespoons olive oil
4 garlic cloves, chopped
1½ pounds tomatoes, skinned (see page 20)
and chopped
4 anchovy fillets, chopped
salt and freshly ground black pepper
1 tablespoon chopped oregano, to garnish

wash the fish steaks under running cold water and pat them dry with absorbent paper towel. Put all the marinade ingredients in a bowl and mix together well.

add the white fish steaks to the marinade, turning them until they are thoroughly coated and glistening with oil. Cover the bowl and leave in a cool place for at least 1 hour.

heat the olive oil in a large skillet. Remove the fish steaks from the marinade and fry gently until they are cooked and golden brown on both sides, turning the fish once during cooking. Remove the steaks from the skillet and keep them warm.

while the fish steaks are cooking, make the tomato sauce. Heat the olive oil in a skillet and sauté the garlic until just golden.

add the tomatoes and chopped anchovies, and cook over medium heat until the tomatoes are reduced to a thick pulpy consistency.

season to taste with salt and pepper. Pour the sauce over the fish and sprinkle with fresh oregano.

Serves 4
Preparation time: *15 minutes, plus 1 hour marinating*
Cooking time: *15 minutes*

Marsala Sole
with Parmesan cheese

The cheese and wine in this recipe make a rich, creamy sauce for the fish. Use the best quality sole, such as lemon sole or Dover sole, or use sand dabs.

flour for dusting
4 medium soles or sand dabs, skinned
6 tablespoons butter
2 tablespoons grated Parmesan cheese
4 tablespoons Fish Broth (see page 11)
3 tablespoons Marsala or dessert white wine
salt and freshly ground black pepper

To serve
grated Parmesan cheese
sprigs of flat-leaved parsley
lemon wedges

put some flour in a shallow bowl and season with salt and pepper. Dip the fish into the seasoned flour to dust them lightly on both sides. Shake off any excess flour.

heat the butter in a large skillet. Add the floured fish and cook over gentle heat until they are golden brown on both sides, turning them once during cooking.

sprinkle the grated Parmesan over the sole and then cook very gently for another 2–3 minutes, until the cheese melts.

add the fish broth and the wine. Cover the pan and cook over very low heat for 4–5 minutes, until the fish are cooked and tender and the sauce reduced. Serve sprinkled with grated Parmesan cheese and garnish with lemon wedges.

Serves 4
Preparation time: *5 minutes*
Cooking time: *12 minutes*

Sicilian Fish Stew
with black olives

Sicily abounds in sardines, tuna, swordfish, gray mullet, and cod. Mussels are also plentiful, and feature in many dishes.

1¼ cups mussels
6 tablespoons olive oil
1 onion, thinly sliced
2 garlic cloves, crushed
2 carrots, cut into strips
1¾ cups canned chopped tomatoes
½ cup black olives
1 bay leaf
4 slices of white bread
2 pounds mixed seafood (e.g. red snapper, redfish, clams, shrimp) prepared or cut into pieces
salt and freshly ground black pepper
2 tablespoons fresh parsley, finely chopped, to garnish

prepare the mussels: cover with cold water and discard any that are open, or rise to the surface. Scrub well to remove any barnacles, remove the beards, and soak in fresh cold water until ready to cook.

heat 2 tablespoons of the olive oil in a heavy-based skillet, and sauté the onion, garlic, and carrots for about 5 minutes or until soft. Add the tomatoes with their juice, black olives, and bay leaf, and season with salt and black pepper. Simmer gently for 15 minutes.

cut four large circles from the slices of bread. Heat the remaining oil in a small skillet and then sauté the bread until crisp and golden on both sides. Remove, drain on absorbent paper towel, and keep warm.

add the prepared fish to the stew and cook for 5 minutes. Add the mussels and simmer for 10 minutes or until the shells open. Discard any that do not open. Remove the bay leaf. Put a piece of fried bread in the bottom of each of 4 warm deep plates or large shallow soup bowls. Ladle the fish stew over the top. Sprinkle with chopped parsley and serve immediately with plenty of crusty bread.

Serves 4
Preparation time: *30 minutes*
Cooking time: *35 minutes*

Jumbo Shrimp
in a cream and mustard sauce

This is a luxuriously rich recipe for which the finest jumbo shrimp should be used, so it is a good choice for special occasions. If you can get it, use Grappa or Italian-style brandy.

¼ cup butter
24 raw jumbo shrimp, shelled
2 tablespoons Grappa or other brandy
1 cup heavy cream
2–3 teaspoons French-style mustard
salt and white pepper

To garnish
1 tablespoon chopped parsley
lemon wedges

heat the butter in a skillet and cook the shrimp for a few minutes. Warm the brandy, pour it over the shrimp, and flambé.

when the flames have subsided, stir in the cream. Season to taste with the mustard, salt, and pepper.

simmer very gently for 4–5 minutes until the shrimp are tender, making sure that they do not become tough.

pour into a hot serving dish and sprinkle with chopped parsley before serving with boiled rice.

Serves 4
Preparation time: *15 minutes*
Cooking time: *12–15 minutes*

clipboard: For a less expensive dish, use 1 pound peeled bay shrimp. In this case, boil the cream first for 4–5 minutes until it thickens slightly. Heat the shrimp in the butter, flambé with brandy, pour the cream over, season to taste with mustard, salt, and pepper, and serve.

Frittura Mista
from the catch of the day

The Adriatic waters yield a variety of fish, so when Italian fishermen get just a few of each kind in their nets, they cook them all together in this typical sea food fry.

4–6 ounces prepared squid (calamari), sliced
4–6 ounces whitebait
4–6 ounces jumbo shrimp
4–6 ounces whitefish fillets, skinned and cut into ½-inch strips
I cup all-purpose flour
salt and pepper
oil for deep frying

To garnish
I–2 lemons, sliced or quartered
few sprigs of flat-leaved parsley

wash all the fish and dry well with absorbent paper towel. Season the flour with salt and pepper.

heat the oil in a deep to 350–375°F or until a 1-inch cube of bread browns in 30 seconds.

toss the fish, a batch at a time, into the seasoned flour and fry until golden brown.

drain well on absorbent paper towel, place on a hot serving dish, and keep hot.

sprinkle the fish lightly with salt and garnish the dish with lemon and parsley just before serving.

Serves 4
Preparation time: *30–40 minutes*
Cooking time: *15–20 minutes*

clipboard: Any selection of small white-fleshed fish or pieces of fish can be used in this dish, such as clams, pieces of red snapper, bluefish, or monkfish, cooked shelled mussels, or small peeled shrimp.

Baked Mussels

with Parmesan and garlic

If you can find good, fresh mussels in the market, try this recipe. It is a typically Italian way of preparing them.

2½ pounds mussels

bouquet garni

½ cup water

½ cup dry white wine

2 tablespoons finely chopped shallot

I garlic clove, crushed

2 tablespoons chopped fresh parsley

6 tablespoons fresh bread crumbs

3 tablespoons grated Parmesan cheese

2 tablespoons butter

salt and freshly ground black pepper

prepare the mussels: place them in a bowl and cover them with cold water. Discard any that are open or rise to the surface. Scrub the mussels to remove any barnacles and remove the beards. Soak in fresh cold water until ready to cook. Drain well.

put the mussels in a deep saucepan with the bouquet garni, salt and pepper. Add the water and wine, cover the pan and cook over moderate heat until the mussels open, shaking the pan occasionally. Discard any mussels that do not open, then strain them and reserve the liquid.

remove the empty half of each mussel shell and arrange the remaining shells close together, mussel side up, in a shallow ovenproof baking dish. Sprinkle the mussels with the chopped shallot, garlic, parsley, bread crumbs, and Parmesan.

reduce the mussel liquid to half its original volume by boiling rapidly. Pour the reduced liquid around the mussels and dot with butter. Bake in a preheated oven at 350°F for 15 minutes. Serve at once.

Serves 4
Preparation time: *30 minutes*
Cooking time: *15–20 minutes*
Oven temperature: *350°F*

Broiled Mussels

with tomatoes and bell peppers

These broiled mussels make a colorful and inexpensive appetizer, and they are really easy and quick to cook.

2 pounds mussels
1 cup dry white wine
½ red bell pepper, seeded and chopped
2 garlic cloves, crushed
4 tablespoons fresh parsley, finely chopped
½ cup chopped tomatoes
5 tablespoons fresh white bread crumbs
2 tablespoons olive oil
1 tablespoon grated Parmesan cheese
salt and freshly ground black pepper
fresh parsley, finely chopped, to garnish

prepare the mussels: cover with cold water and discard any that are open, or rise to the surface. Scrub them under running cold water to remove any barnacles and the beards. Put the cleaned mussels in a large saucepan with the wine and bring to a boil, covered with a close-fitting lid.

cook the mussels over medium heat for a few minutes, still covered. Shake the pan occasionally until the mussels open. Discard any mussels that do not open. Remove the open mussels from the pan and take off and throw away the top half of each shell.

mix together the chopped pepper, garlic, parsley, chopped tomatoes, and 4 tablespoons of the bread crumbs in a bowl. Stir in 1 tablespoon of the olive oil and then season to taste with salt and freshly ground black pepper.

add a little of this mixture to each of the mussels in their shells and place them in an ovenproof dish. Sprinkle with grated Parmesan and the remaining bread crumbs and olive oil. Bake in a preheated oven at 150°F for 10 minutes. Preheat the boiler to hot and briefly broil the mussels for a crisp finish. Sprinkle with parsley.

Serves 4–6
Preparation time: *30 minutes*
Cooking time: *10 minutes*
Oven temperature: *150°F*

Pasta and Gnocchi

Fresh pasta

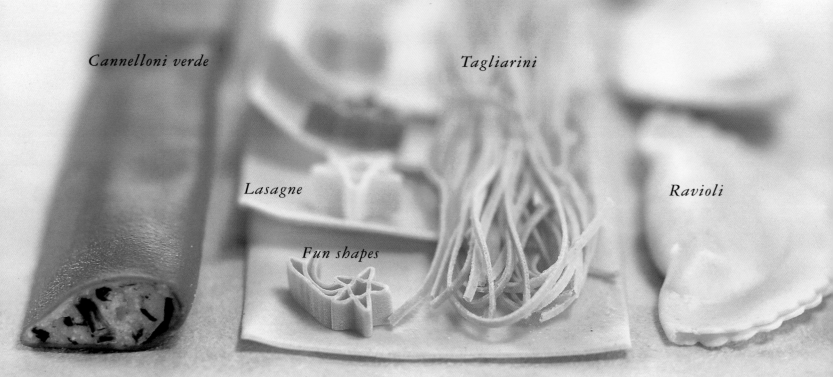

Cannelloni verde

Tagliarini

Lasagne

Ravioli

Fun shapes

Cannelloni verde
Cannelloni consists of large, thin tubes of pasta which can be stuffed with a variety of different ingredients and served with a cheese sauce. It is often made with spinach, which colors it green .

Lasagne
Lasagne is very popular, and is made in flat, broad sheets which are available fresh or dried. The sheets are usually cooked and layered with meat, cheese, vegetables, and sauce and baked in the oven.

Fun shapes
These are particularly appealing to children and are great for parties.

Tagliarini
Tagliarini consists of long, flat, ribbon-shaped noodles

rolled paper thin. They are often used in soups.

Ravioli
Ravioli is very popular. Two shapes of pasta are parceled together and stuffed with meat, cheese or vegetables.

Tortelloni

Linguine Verde

Caramelle

Agnolini

Cappelletti

and covered in a sauce. It is usually made in a half-moon shape when made at home in Italy. Fresh ravioli is best.

Caramelle
This fresh pasta is made in the shape of a sweet, often encasing a delicious stuffing such as a mixture of spinach and ricotta cheese.

Tortelloni
Tortelloni is pinched into shapes which look like small ears. It is mostly stuffed with spinach and ricotta, and is served like ravioli with a sauce or with butter and freshly ground pepper.

Agnolini
Agnolini is another pasta used with various stuffings. The small crescent shapes are cooked, then served with a meat or cream sauce.

Linguine Verde
Linguine is available fresh or dried, it is a flat ribbon noodle similar to fettucine.

Cappelletti
The "little hats" can be filled with any suitable stuffing such as spinach, ricotta etc.

Fresh Pasta

to make at home

This makes a standard quantity of home-made fresh pasta.

2½ cups all-purpose flour, sifted

pinch of salt

3 eggs

1 tablespoon of olive oil

flour for dusting

put the flour and salt on a work surface. Make a well in the center and add the eggs. Using the fingertips, draw the flour in from the sides and mix well. Add the olive oil and continue mixing until you have a soft dough. Alternatively, you can make the dough in a food processor.

turn out the dough on to a lightly floured surface and knead well until it is really smooth and silky. Roll out the dough, giving it an occasional quarter turn and stretching it out until it resembles a thick sheet of cloth and is almost transparent.

hang the pasta over the back of a chair or a broom handle and leave to dry for about 10 minutes. Alternatively, lay it out on a table with one-third overhanging the edge, and keep turning it so that it dries out completely.

roll up the pasta loosely like a jellyroll and then cut through horizontally at regular intervals to make fettuccine (⅛ inch wide) or tagliatelle (¼ inch wide). Unravel the strands and toss gently in a little flour. Leave them to dry on a cloth for at least 30 minutes before cooking in salted boiling water. Serve with a sauce or simply tossed with olive oil, garlic, salt and pepper and parsley.

Serves 4
Preparation time: *1 hour*
Cooking time: *2–3 minutes*

clipboard: To make lasagne or ravioli, cut the prepared pasta dough into sheets, as required, rather than strips.

Deep-fried Pasta
from Tuscany

This is a traditional pasta recipe from the heart of Italy. These crisp, tasty puffs make excellent tidbits to serve with drinks, and are great with savory sauces and dips.

½ teaspoon dry yeast
¼ teaspoon sugar
4 cups all-purpose flour
2 tablespoons butter
⅔ cup lukewarm Chicken Broth
(see page 11)
vegetable oil for deep frying
salt and freshly ground black pepper

dissolve the yeast and sugar in a little water. Set aside for 10 minutes.

sift the flour and a little salt on to a work surface. Stir in the yeast mixture, then add the butter and enough broth to make a soft dough. Knead well, then roll out to a fairly thick sheet.

fold the 4 corners of the dough in towards the center, then flatten with the rolling pin.

fold and flatten again at least 5 more times. Roll out to a sheet about ¼ inch thick and cut into small rectangles.

deep-fry the shapes a few at a time in hot oil until golden brown and puffed up. Drain on absorbent paper towels while frying the remainder. Sprinkle with salt and pepper, and serve hot.

Serves 6
Preparation time: *1 hour, plus 10 minutes resting*
Cooking time: *20–30 minutes, depending on the number of batches*

Penne
with chili sauce

*Pasta with chili sauce is a true Italian classic.
This recipe is not too hot, and once you've
got used to the intense flavor of the
chili peppers, you'll really enjoy it.*

1–2 tablespoons olive oil
1 large onion, finely chopped
2 garlic cloves, crushed
4 slices rindless bacon, chopped
1–2 fresh red chili peppers, chopped
1 x 14-ounce can chopped tomatoes
2–4 ounces pecorino or Parmesan cheese
1 pound penne
salt and pepper

heat the oil in a skillet and cook the onion, garlic, and bacon, until they are lightly colored.

add the chili peppers, and tomatoes. Grate one quarter of the cheese and add it. Season to taste with salt and pepper. Cook over a gentle heat for 30–40 minutes until the sauce thickens. Check the seasoning.

cook the penne in boiling salted water for about 12 minutes until just tender (*al dente*). Drain well and place in a hot serving dish.

stir in most of the sauce, mix well and then pour the remaining sauce over the top. Shave a quarter of the remaining pecorino or Parmesan cheese into curls and use to decorate the dish. Grate the rest and serve it separately.

Serves 4
Preparation time: *15–20 minutes*
Cooking time: *50 minutes–1 hour*

clipboard: You can use either red or green chili peppers, the red ones being hotter. For a milder taste, slice the chili peppers in half lengthwise and scrape out the seeds with the point of a small knife before chopping them. Be careful not to touch your eyes or mouth and wash your hands well after handling chili peppers as the juice is very pungent.

Trenette
with anchovies and tomatoes

The anchovies in this recipe make a perfect blend with the peppers and tomatoes. It is an ideal dish to make from ingredients on hand.

4–6 tablespoons olive oil
2 garlic cloves, crushed
2 large onions, finely chopped
1 red pepper, skinned, seeded and cut into strips
1¾ cups canned chopped plum tomatoes
1½ ounce canned anchovies, drained and chopped
pinch of sugar
1 pound trenette
8 tablespoons grated Parmesan cheese
salt and pepper
1 tablespoon minced parsley, to garnish

heat half the oil in a pan and cook the garlic and onions until soft and just beginning to color.

add the pepper strips and cook until soft, then add the tomatoes and anchovies, season with pepper, and stir in the sugar. Cook for a few minutes longer until the tomatoes and anchovies are heated through.

meanwhile, cook the trenette in boiling salted water for about 7 minutes until just tender (*al dente*) Drain well.

place in a hot serving dish and stir in a little sauce, half the cheese and, if you wish, the remaining oil.

pour over the rest of the sauce just before serving, and sprinkle the chopped parsley over the top. Serve the remaining grated cheese separately.

Serves 4
Preparation time: *15–20 minutes*
Cooking time: *40 minutes*

clipboard: To remove the skin from a pepper, place the halved or quartered pepper under a moderately hot broiler and cook until the skin starts to blacken and curl. Then scrape the skin off with a sharp knife.

Spaghetti *with sardines, anchovies, and fennel*

Try this unusual pasta sauce — it's a special treat.

1 head fennel, quartered
8–10 tablespoons olive oil
2 garlic cloves, crushed
1 pound fresh sardines or other small fish
2 large onions, finely sliced
1 tablespoon yellow raisins
1 tablespoon pine nuts (pignolas)
6 anchovy fillets, chopped
2 tablespoons minced parsley
⅔ cup white wine or Fish Broth (see page 11)
1 pound spaghetti
white bread crumbs, lightly browned
salt and freshly ground black pepper

cook the fennel in boiling salted water until almost tender. Drain well, reserving the cooking liquid. Chop the fennel coarsely.

heat 3 tablespoons oil in a pan and add the garlic. Cook gently until golden brown then add the sardines and cook gently for an additional 10 minutes.

meanwhile, heat another 3 tablespoons of oil in a pan and cook the onions until they are soft and golden brown.

add the fennel, yellow raisins, pine nuts, anchovies, parsley, and wine or fish broth. Season lightly. Cook over a moderate heat for 10 minutes.

cook the spaghetti in boiling salted water to which the fennel water has been added. Drain well and place half in an oven–to-table dish. Cover with half the sardines and a little of the onions and fennel.

repeat the layers and sprinkle breadcrumbs and a little oil over the top. Cook in a preheated oven at 400° F, for 20 minutes.
Serve immediately, sprinkled with freshly ground black pepper.

Serves 4
Preparation time: *10 minutes*
Cooking time: *1 hour*
Oven temperature: *400° F*

clipboard: To prepare the sardines, bone them and remove the heads and tails. Cut each sardine into 2 or 3 pieces, depending on size, before cooking them.

Spaghetti alla Carbonara

This is a delightful way of using the familiar ingredients of egg and bacon in an authentic Italian dish.

1 pound spaghetti
8 slices bacon
2 tablespoons olive oil
3 eggs, beaten
3 tablespoons light cream
4 tablespoons Parmesan cheese, grated
2 tablespoons chopped
fresh parsley, finely chopped, to garnish (optional)
salt and freshly ground black pepper

bring a pan of salted water to a boil, adding a little oil if wished to prevent the spaghetti sticking together.

when the water reaches a rolling boil, add the spaghetti to the pan and continue boiling until it is cooked through but still firm to the bite (*al dente*) Drain well.

while the spaghetti is cooking, chop the bacon into small pieces and sauté it in the olive oil in a large heavy-based saucepan until cooked and golden brown.

add the drained cooked spaghetti to the pan and gently stir in the beaten eggs, salt, freshly ground black pepper, and cream.

stir very gently over a low heat until the egg starts to set.

toss the spaghetti mixture lightly with most of the Parmesan and serve immediately while still very hot, sprinkled with the remaining Parmesan and the minced parsley, if using.

Serves:4
Preparation time: *5 minutes*
Cooking time: *15–20 minutes*

Spaghetti alla Bolognese

This is one of countless meat and vegetable sauces that are served with pasta. The beautiful city of Bologna is renowned for its fine pasta, and is the birthplace of several classic Italian recipes.

Meat sauce

4 tablespoons olive oil

I onion, minced

I garlic clove, crushed

4 slices bacon, chopped

I carrot, diced

I celery stick, diced

I pound lean ground beef

⅔ cup red wine

½ cup milk

grated nutmeg

1¾ cups chopped tomatoes

I tablespoon sugar

I teaspoon chopped fresh oregano

salt and freshly ground black pepper

I pound spaghetti

I teaspoon olive oil

freshly ground black pepper

4 tablespoons Parmesan cheese, grated, to garnish (optional)

make the sauce: heat the oil in a saucepan or deep skillet and sauté the onion, garlic, bacon, carrot, and celery until soft and golden. Add the beef and cook, stirring occasionally, until browned.

add the red wine and bring to a boil. Reduce the heat slightly and cook over medium heat until most of the wine has evaporated. Season with salt and freshly ground black pepper.

add the milk and a little grated nutmeg, and stir well. Continue cooking until the milk has been absorbed by the meat mixture. Add the tomatoes, sugar, and oregano. Reduce the heat to a bare simmer and cook, uncovered for 2–2½ hours until the sauce is reduced and richly colored.

bring a large saucepan of salted water to the boil. Add the spaghetti and olive oil and cook until tender but firm to the bite (*al dente*). Drain well and season with freshly ground black pepper. Pour over the meat sauce and serve the Parmesan separately.

Serves 4
Preparation time: *10 minutes*
Cooking time: *2½–3 hours*

Spaghetti alle Vongole

This is the perfect recipe to cook when clams are at their best. Try to use small clams, such as littlenecks, Manila clams, or New Zealand cockles.

2 pounds fresh clams, scrubbed and cleaned (see clipboard below)
7 tablespoons water
7 tablespoons olive oil
1 garlic clove, peeled and sliced
4 medium tomatoes, skinned (see page 20) and mashed
4 ounces spaghetti
salt and freshly ground black pepper
1 tablespoon chopped parsley

put the clams in a large pan with the water. Cook until the shells open, then remove the clams from the shells. Strain the cooking liquid and reserve for later.

heat the oil in a heavy pan, add the garlic and simmer gently for 5 minutes. Remove the garlic, then add the tomatoes and the reserved cooking liquid to the pasta. Stir and simmer for 20 minutes.

meanwhile, cook the spaghetti in plenty of boiling salted water until tender but firm to the bite (*al dente*). Drain thoroughly.

add the clams and parsley to the tomato sauce and heat thoroughly for 1 minute. Pile the spaghetti in a warmed serving dish, add the sauce and a pinch of pepper and fork gently to mix. Serve immediately.

Serves 4
Preparation time: *10 minutes*
Cooking time: *40 minutes*

clipboard: Fresh clams in their shells should be well scrubbed and washed before heating. To check if they are alive and well, tap the shell briskly — the clam should immediately respond by shutting tightly.

Tagliatelle
with tomato and basil sauce

A deceptively simple yet beautifully flavored sauce to serve with pasta. Tomatoes, basil, and olives are generously combined to produce a full, vibrant taste.

4 tablespoons olive oil
2 onions, chopped
2 garlic cloves, crushed
4 plum tomatoes, skinned (see page 20) and chopped
2 tablespoons tomato paste
1 teaspoon sugar
⅓ cup dry white wine
few ripe olives, pitted and quartered
handful of torn basil leaves
12 ounces dried tagliatelle
salt and freshly ground black pepper
2 ounces Parmesan cheese, shaved

heat 3 tablespoons of the olive oil in a large skillet. Add the onions and garlic, and sauté gently over low heat until they are soft and slightly colored. Stir the mixture occasionally.

add the tomatoes, tomato paste, sugar, and wine, stirring well. Cook over gentle heat until the mixture is quite thick and reduced. Stir in the quartered olives and torn basil leaves, and season to taste with salt and plenty of freshly ground black pepper.

meanwhile, add the tagliatelle to a large pan of boiling salted water (to which a little oil has been added to prevent the pasta sticking together). Boil rapidly until the tagliatelle is tender but still firm to the bite (*al dente*).

drain the tagliatelle immediately, mixing in the remaining olive oil and a generous grinding of black pepper. Arrange the pasta on 4 serving plates and top with the tomato sauce, mixing it into the tagliatelle. Serve with large curls of shaved Parmesan.

Serves 4
Preparation time: *10 minutes*
Cooking time: *20 minutes*

Tagliatelle
with beans and sage

Sage (salvia in Italian) is widely used in Italian cooking, and imparts a pungent flavor. It combines very well with the beans, bacon, wine and olive oil in this recipe.

3 tablespoons olive oil

3 slices smoked bacon, derinded and cubed

1 onion, finely chopped

5 sage leaves

1 cup canned pinto or cannellini beans

2 tablespoons Chicken Broth (see page 11)

¼ teaspoon all-purpose flour

1 tablespoon tomato paste

2 tablespoons red wine

14 ounces tagliatelle

2 tablespoons Parmesan cheese, grated

1 tablespoon pecorino cheese, grated

extra sage leaves to garnish (optional)

heat the oil in a large, heavy-based skillet. Add the bacon, onion, and whole sage leaves. Cook over a medium heat until golden.

drain the beans, rinse, and drain again, then add to the pan.

heat the broth. Mix the flour and tomato paste in a small bowl; stir in the hot broth and the wine.

pour into the bean mixture, stir with a wooden spoon, and simmer over a low heat until the sauce thickens.

cook the pasta in plenty of lightly salted boiling water until tender but firm to the bite (*al dente*).

remove the sage leaves from the sauce, taste, and adjust the seasoning. Drain the pasta, mix with the sauce and put in a large heated serving dish. Add the Parmesan and pecorino, and serve hot, garnished with a few fresh sage leaves if desired.

Serves 4
Preparation time: *10 minutes*
Cooking time: *30 minutes*

Linguine
with mussels in tomato sauce

10 cups mussels
3 tablespoons olive oil
1 onion, chopped
3 garlic cloves, crushed
6 medium tomatoes, skinned (see page 20) and chopped
1 pound linguine
salt and freshly ground black pepper
3 tablespoons fresh parsley, chopped

prepare the mussels as follows: cover them with cold water and discard any that open or float to the surface. Scrub the remaining mussels and remove the beards.

place in a large saucepan with ⅓ cup water, cover with a lid, and cook over moderate heat until the mussels open, shaking the pan occasionally. Drain the mussels and remove the shells, leaving a few in their shells to garnish. Discard any that do not open.

heat the olive oil in a skillet and add the onion and garlic. Sauté over medium heat until golden and tender.

add the chopped tomatoes, season, then cook gently over low heat until the mixture is thickened and reduced.

add the shelled mussels and mix gently into the tomato sauce. Simmer over low heat for 2–3 minutes or until the mussels are heated through.

cook the linguine in salted boiling water until it is tender but firm to the bite (*al dente*). Drain well and gently toss with the tomato and mussel sauce.

transfer to a serving dish or 4 warm plates. Sprinkle with chopped parsley and garnish with the reserved mussels.

Serves 4
Preparation time: *25 minutes*
Cooking time: *20 minutes*

Mushroom Ravioli

Ravioli is mostly shaped into crescents or circles when made at home, but whatever shape you choose, you'll enjoy the taste.

2 tablespoons olive oil
1 onion, minced
1–2 garlic cloves, crushed
4 cups finely chopped mushrooms
1 cup ricotta cheese
1 egg, beaten
2–3 tablespoons white bread crumbs
1 x quantity egg pasta dough (see page 64)
⅓ cup butter
salt and freshly ground pepper
4 tablespoons grated Parmesan cheese

heat the oil, add the onion and garlic, and cook gently until soft and lightly colored. Add the mushrooms and continue to cook gently until the mushrooms are soft and any liquid has evaporated.

remove from the heat, beat in the ricotta and egg, and sufficient bread crumbs to give a firm mixture. Season to taste.

roll out the pasta dough thinly and cut out 2½ inch rounds. Place a portion of the mixture on each, brush around the edge of the dough with cold water, fold over and seal. Alternatively, cut out 1 inch square or round shapes, place the filling in the center, brush around the edge of the dough with cold water, top with a matching shape, and seal.

cook a few ravioli at a time for 4–5 minutes in boiling salted water. They are cooked when they rise to the surface. Remove with a slotted spoon, drain well, and place in a hot serving platter. Cover and keep hot until all the ravioli are cooked. Just before serving, heat the butter in a skillet until it is a light golden brown, and pour immediately over the ravioli. Sprinkle a little of the Parmesan over the top and serve the rest separately. Serve hot with freshly ground black pepper.

Serves 4
Preparation time: *30 minutes*
Cooking time: *30 minutes*

Dry pasta

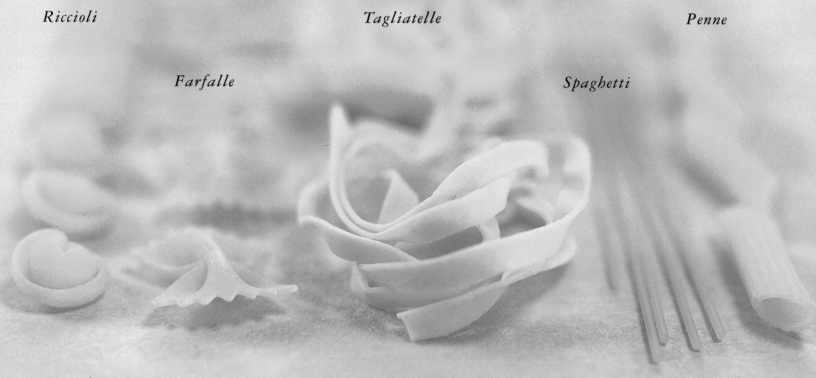

Riccioli

Farfalle

Tagliatelle

Spaghetti

Penne

Riccioli
Riccioli is similar in shape to the ready-stuffed pasta called cappeletti (which means "little hats"). It is sold in dry form and has no filling. It is useful for holding morsels of food in the pasta sauce.

Farfalle
Farfalle is a delightful pasta which is made in different sized butterfly shapes — the pasta is pinched to form pretty butterflies/bow ties. It looks very attractive when served with a colorful sauce and garnished.

Tagliatelle
Tagliatelle is a very popular pasta which can be bought fresh or dried. It is very similar to fettucine but is slightly thinner and wider. It is served with all the classic pasta sauces.

Spaghetti
Spaghetti is probably the best known and most popular of all the pastas and can be bought fresh or dried. The long, thin rod-like pasta is generally associated with the famous bolognese sauce.

Penne
Penne is a hollow, quill-like pasta, as the name implies, which has diagonal tips to its tubes. It is a very popular, versatile pasta, and can be bought dried or fresh. Penne is boiled until just tender (*al dente*) and served with all of the classic pasta sauces.

Rigatoni

Spirali

Conchiglie

Fiorelli

Casareccie

Conchiglie

Conchiglie consists of small, pretty, dried shells of pasta. "Conchiglie" means little conches or shells. As with other similarly-shaped pasta, it is often served with sauces containing ground meat. This is because the convenient little hollows in the shells tend to trap the meat as well as the sauce.

Rigatoni

Rigatoni is a very popular pasta made in the form of ridged, hollow tubes. They are ideal for baking in a rich sauce. Alternatively, they can be boiled until they are just tender (*al dente*) then tossed in a meaty pasta sauce. Like conchiglie they are very good for retaining the meat and vegetable sauce.

Fiorelli

Fiorelli is a one of the few pasta shapes meant to resemble a flower. It is round and curly, and makes an attractive alternative to the more common pasta shapes. Fiorelli should be cooked until it is just tender (*al dente*) and served with the pasta sauce and garnish of your choice.

Spirali

This spiral-shaped, dried pasta, should be cooked and served with a sauce of the cook's choice.

Casareccie

This small, twisted pasta originates from Sicily. It is made in long, thin strips, which are then twisted to create an interesting shape.

Baked Lasagne

with a savory meat sauce

This baked lasagne dish is warming and tasty. It is substantial enough to serve on its own, piping hot, accompanied by a robust red wine and a fresh salad.

⅔–¾ cup milk
2 cups béchamel sauce (see clipboard below)
salt and white pepper
1 x quantity Meat Sauce (see page 77), cooked for 20 minutes only
8 ounces quick-cook dried green or white lasagne, or fresh pasta cut into thin 7½ x 3½ inch sheets
12 ounces Bel Paese or Fontina cheese, thinly sliced or shredded
2–3 tablespoons grated Parmesan
sprig of fresh basil, to garnish

whisk sufficient milk into the béchamel sauce to make a thin creamy consistency. Check the seasoning.

butter an oven-to-table dish. Starting with a little meat sauce, layer the meat sauce, lasagne, béchamel sauce and Bel Paese or Fontina in the dish, ending with a layer of béchamel sauce.

sprinkle the Parmesan over the top and bake in a preheated oven at 350°F for 40–45 minutes. Serve hot, garnished with a sprig of fresh basil.

Serves 4
Preparation time: *15–20 minutes*
Cooking time: *40–45 minutes*
Oven Temperature: *350°F*

clipboard: To make béchamel sauce: melt 3 tablespoons butter and stir in 3 tablespoons flour. Cook over gentle heat for 2–3 minutes, and gradually beat in 2 cups milk, stirring constantly, until you have a thick, smooth, glossy sauce. Season with salt, pepper, and a little nutmeg.

Layered Pasta
with a Parmesan and meat sauce

A hearty meat sauce is blended with Parmesan and butter, resulting in a really wholesome baked lasagne.

1 x quantity Meat Sauce (see page 77)

Béchamel sauce

3 tablespoons butter
3 tablespoons flour
2½ cups milk
pinch of ground nutmeg
salt and freshly ground black pepper

8 ounces quick-cook dried lasagne sheets, or freshly made lasagne
4 tablespoons grated Parmesan cheese
1 tablespoon butter

make the meat sauce, and simmer gently for at least 1 hour until it is time to assemble the lasagne.

make the béchamel sauce: melt the butter in a saucepan and stir in the flour. Cook over gentle heat, without browning, for 2–3 minutes and then gradually beat in the milk until you have a thick, smooth glossy sauce. Season with nutmeg, salt, and pepper, and cook gently for 5–10 minutes.

put a little of the meat sauce in a buttered ovenproof dish and cover with a layer of lasagne and then another layer of meat sauce, topped with some béchamel sauce. Continue layering up in this way, ending with a layer of lasagne and a topping of béchamel.

sprinkle with grated Parmesan and then dot the top with butter. Bake in a preheated oven at 450°F for 30 minutes, until the lasagne is golden brown.

Serves 4
Preparation time: *1¼ hours*
Cooking time: *30 minutes*
Oven temperature: *450°F*

Penne
with a spicy sausage sauce

The best sausage to use in this recipe is a spicy Italian variety like salamelle. The fresh vegetables add a lovely, clean-flavored taste to the pasta sauce.

3 tablespoons oil
2 tablespoons butter
½ onion, minced
½ small shallot, minced
1 small carrot, finely sliced
1 celery stalk, sliced
4 ounces salamelle sausage, crumbled
½ small yellow bell pepper, seeded and diced
4 basil leaves, torn
4 tablespoons dry red wine
14 ounces penne
2 tablespoons grated pecorino cheese
2 tablespoons grated Parmesan cheese
few whole basil leaves, to garnish

heat the oil and butter in a flameproof casserole, add the onion, shallot, carrot, and celery, and cook over low heat for 4 minutes.

mix well then add the crumbled sausage, diced pepper, and torn basil. Brown over medium heat for 3–4 minutes, and moisten with red wine.

cook the penne in lightly salted boiling water until tender but firm to the bite (*al dente*), and drain.

transfer the penne to a heated serving dish and pour on the sausage and vegetable sauce.

sprinkle with the cheeses and mix well before serving, garnished with whole basil leaves.

Serves 4
Preparation time: *10 minutes*
Cooking time: *10 minutes*

clipboard: Look around specialist Italian food stores or the delicatessen counters of supermarkets to find the spicy salamelle cooking sausage. If you can't find it, use another spicy sausage, such as chorizo.

Macaroni

with anchovies and garlic

This is how macaroni is prepared country-style in Italian households. The anchovies and olives provide a distinctly salty tang to the sauce.

2 anchovy fillets

a little milk

4 tablespoons oil

1 garlic clove

2 slices smoked bacon, derinded and diced

1¾ cups plum tomatoes

4 tablespoons pitted black olives, chopped

¼ teaspoon chopped oregano

12 ounces macaroni

2 tablespoons grated pecorino cheese

salt and pepper

soak the anchovy fillets in a little milk to remove excess salt.

heat the oil in a small pan. Add the whole garlic clove and the drained anchovies. Cook over medium heat for a few minutes, then remove the garlic and add the bacon.

meanwhile, drain the tomatoes and cut into strips. When the bacon is crisp, add the tomatoes to the pan. Season with salt and pepper and leave to cook over low heat for about 20 minutes until the liquid thickens. Add the olives and oregano halfway through the cooking time.

cook the pasta in a large pan of lightly salted boiling water until tender but firm to the bite (*al dente*).

drain and transfer to a heated serving dish, then pour on the sauce and sprinkle with the grated pecorino cheese. Mix well before serving.

Serves 4
Preparation time: *10 minutes*
Cooking time: *30 minutes*

Roman Gnocchi
baked with Parmesan

Gnocchi are mouthwatering to eat, and great fun to prepare. They can be made either from potato or, as in this recipe, from farina (cream of wheat.)

2½ cups milk
½ cup farina (cream of wheat)
pinch of nutmeg
½ cup Gruyère grated cheese
4 tablespoons melted butter
2–4 tablespoons Parmesan cheese, grated
salt and white pepper

bring the milk to a boil. Remove from the heat and immediately add the farina (cream of wheat) all at once. Beat well until smooth, season with a pinch of nutmeg, salt, and pepper.

return to the heat, bring to a boil and cook for 5–7 minutes over moderate heat, beating vigorously all the time until the mixture leaves the sides of the pan. Beat in the Gruyère and check the seasoning.

turn out the mixture on to a buttered or oiled baking tray and spread into a sheet approximately ½–¾ inch thick. Leave until cold, then refrigerate until completely firm.

cut the gnocchi into rounds with a 2–2 ½ inch pastry cutter. Arrange, overlapping, in a buttered ovenproof dish. (Re-form any leftover mixture and cut out more rounds.) Pour the melted butter over the top and sprinkle with the Parmesan. Bake in a preheated oven at 425°F for 20–30 minutes until golden brown. Serve straight from the oven

Serves 4–6
Preparation time: *20–30 minutes, plus firming*
Cooking time: *30–40 minutes*
Oven temperature: *425°F*

clipboard: To make this dish more substantial, cut 6 slices bacon into strips. Fry them gently in a little oil and sprinkle over the gnocchi in the baking dish.

Potato Gnocchi
with tomato sauce

Tomato sauce
3 tablespoons olive oil
1¾ cups chopped tomatoes
1 teaspoon dried oregano
pinch sugar
salt and freshly ground black pepper

Gnocchi
1½ pounds russet (floury) potatoes, peeled and cut
into
even-sized pieces
1¾–2 cups all-purpose flour
2 egg yolks, beaten
pinch of nutmeg
4-6 tablespoons melted butter
4 tablespoons Parmesan cheese, grated
salt and white pepper

make the tomato sauce: put all the ingredients in a pan and bring to a boil. Simmer briskly, uncovered, for 20–25 minutes, until the sauce is thick. Serve hot or cold as preferred.

cook the potatoes in boiling salted water until tender. Drain well and return to the heat for a few moments, shaking the pan all the time to dry out the potatoes. Sieve the potatoes through a vegetable mill or mash until smooth. Beat in most of the flour and the egg yolks, add the nutmeg, and mix until well blended.

turn out onto a floured board and knead in more flour, if necessary, to give a firm mixture. Roll out the potato mixture into finger lengths about ½ inch in diameter and cut into 1¼ inch pieces. Press the center of each piece lightly between thumb and forefinger or with a fork to flatten them slightly.

cook the gnocchi, a few at a time, in a large pan of gently boiling water. They are cooked when they rise to the surface. Remove with a slotted spoon and drain well.

place the cooked gnocchi in a warn, buttered serving dish and keep hot until all the gnocchi are cooked. Before serving, pour the hot melted butter over them. Sprinkle with a little Parmesan, and serve the rest separately with fresh tomato sauce.

Serves 4
Preparation time: *20–30 minutes*
Cooking time: *30–40 minutes*

Baked Macaroni
with fresh shrimp

Béchamel sauce
2 tablespoons butter
2 tablespooons all-purpose flour
1¼ cups milk
pinch of ground nutmeg
salt and freshly ground black pepper

⅓ cup butter
¾ cup button mushrooms, sliced
1 cup peeled shrimp
2 tablespoons warmed brandy
4–6 tablespoons Parmesan cheese, grated
8 ounces short macaroni
sprigs of fresh basil, to garnish

make 1¼ cups bechamel sauce (see page 90). Keep warm.

heat half the butter in a skillet and cook the mushrooms until tender. Season to taste with salt and pepper.

add the shrimp and heat through, then pour on the warmed brandy and flambe. When the flames have subsided, stir in half the cheese and check the seasoning.

meanwhile, cook the pasta in boiling salted water until just tender but still firm to the bite (*al dente*). Drain well. Check the seasoning of the béchamel sauce, and add a pinch of nutmeg and the remaining cheese.

place one-third of the macaroni in a buttered oven-to-table dish and spread with half the mushroom mixture. Repeat the layers, ending with a layer of macaroni.

cover with the béchamel sauce. Heat the remaining butter in a pan and, when it is lightly colored, pour it over the top. Bake in a preheated oven at 400°F for about 20 minutes until golden brown. Serve hot, garnished with fresh basil.

Serves 4
Preparation time: *15–20minutes*
Cooking time: *35-40 minutes*
Oven temperature:*400°F*

clipboard: For a more economical dish, you can use cod or smoked haddock which has been skinned, poached in water and broken into chunks with a fork.

Pork, Beef, and Lamb

Loin of Pork
with juniper and bay leaves

2 tablespoons olive oil
2–2½ pounds loin of pork, rind removed,
boned and rolled
1 tablespoon juniper berries, coarsely crushed
2 cloves
10 bay leaves (fresh if possible) plus a sprig to garnish
2 large onions, chopped
1¼ cups dry white wine
⅔–2 cups Chicken Broth (see page 11)
salt and freshly ground black pepper

heat the olive oil in a heavy-based pot or flameproof casserole, just large enough to hold the meat. Brown the meat on all sides.

add the juniper berries, cloves, bay leaves, and onions, and stir into the oil.

season to taste with salt and pepper and pour on the white wine.

cover with a piece of parchment paper and a tight-fitting lid and cook very gently for 1½ hours or until tender.

avoid removing the lid too often but check once or twice while the meat is cooking, adding a little broth if necessary.

remove the meat from the pan, and place on a serving platter. Cover and keep warm.

add sufficient broth to the pan to absorb all the browned residue in the cooking liquid. Bring to a boil, check the seasoning, and strain the liquid. if desired, pour a little over the meat, serving the rest separately. Serve hot, garnished with a fresh bay sprig.

Serves 4–6
Preparation time: *10 minutes*
Cooking time: *1½–2 hours*

clipboard: If you prefer, cook the meat in a preheated moderate oven at 350°F. Take care that the parchment paper does not hang over the sides of the pan by more than ½ inch. Too much paper could be a fire hazard, especially near a gas flame.

Milanese Stew

with pork loin and sausage links

This hearty casserole is full of juicy, meaty flavor. Eat it with plenty of crusty bread to mop up the sauce.

10 ounces pork rind
2 tablespoons butter
3–4 tablespoons olive oil
2 large onions, sliced
2 large carrots, sliced
2 sticks celery, chopped
1¼ pounds lean boneless pork, diced
⅓ cup dry white wine
1½ quarts Chicken Broth (see page 11)
8 ounces Italian-style pork sausage links, cut into 1-inch slices
1 head Savoy cabbage, trimmed and shredded
salt and pepper

place the pork rind in a pan, cover with water, and salt lightly. Bring to a boil and cook for 10 minutes. Drain and cut the rind into 2 inch x ½ inch strips.

heat the butter and half the oil in another pan. Cook the onion until soft but without color, then add the carrots and celery, and cook for about 5 minutes, stirring frequently.

take the vegetables from the pan. Heat the remaining oil and cook the pork until it is no longer pink on the outside, turning frequently. Return the vegetables and pork rind to the pan and pour on the white wine and broth. Season to taste with salt and pepper.

simmer gently for 1½–2 hours until the meat is almost tender. Add the sausage links and cabbage, and cook for an additional 25–30 minutes. Taste and adjust the seasoning, and transfer to a serving dish. Serve hot.

Serves 4–6
Preparation time: *20–25 minutes*
Cooking time: *2–2½ hours*

clipboard: Make this dish the day before you eat it, as standing improves the flavor. Refrigerate it when cold and reheat for 40 minutes over a low heat the following day.

Venetian Beef
in an aromatic, spiced marinade

Gentle simmering in wine and marsala adds complex flavors to this exquisite dish.

1¼ cups red wine vinegar
1 garlic clove, chopped
2 cloves
pinch of cinnamon
2 carrots, chopped
2 sticks celery, chopped
1 sprig each rosemary and thyme
6 tablespoons butter
3–3½ pounds eye round or tenderloin
1 large onion, chopped
1¼ cups dry white wine
1¼ cups Marsala
salt and freshly ground pepper
fresh herbs, to garnish

mix together the vinegar, garlic, cloves, cinnamon, carrots, celery, and herbs, and season well. Place the meat in a deep, non-metal dish and pour the marinade over it. Cover and refrigerate for 12 hours, turning the meat at regular intervals.

drain the meat and vegetables and dry them on absorbent paper towel. Discard the liquid.

heat the butter in a heavy-based pan and cook the onion, carrots, and celery until soft. Remove the vegetables from the pan and add the meat. Brown well on all sides. Return the vegetables to the pan with the wine, Marsala, and salt and pepper to taste. Cover the pan with a piece of parchment paper and a tight-fitting lid, and cook over gentle heat for 2–2½ hours until the meat is tender.

cut the meat into thick slices and arrange on a hot dish. Check the seasoning and strain the sauce over the meat. Sprinkle with black pepper, and garnish with fresh herbs.

> Serves 6–8
> Preparation time: *25–30 minutes, plus marinating*
> Cooking time: *2¼–2¾ hours*

clipboard: To prepare the meat, remove all fat and retie into a compact shape, using butcher's string. This dish is traditionally eaten with polenta, a staple food of northern Italy (see page 180).

Bistecche *topped with a spicy pizzaiolo sauce*

This dish gets its name because the steak is given a pizza-like topping of tomatoes, garlic, and oregano. You can also cook pork chops or hamburgers the same way.

6 tablespoons olive oil
1–2 garlic cloves, crushed
4 tomatoes, peeled and chopped, or
1¾ cups chopped canned tomatoes
1 teaspoon fresh chopped oregano or ½ teaspoon dried oregano
4 x 8-ounce beef steaks, thinly cut, trimmed of all fat
salt and pepper

heat three-quarters of the oil in a pan and cook the garlic gently until golden brown. Add the tomatoes and season lightly with salt, pepper, and oregano.

bring to a boil and simmer for 10–15 minutes until the sauce thickens slightly. Canned tomatoes will take longer than fresh ones.

meanwhile, heat the remaining oil in a skillet and quickly brown the meat on both sides. Pour the sauce over it and continue cooking very gently for 10–15 minutes or until the meat is tender. If necessary, add a little water to prevent the sauce reducing too much.

arrange the steaks on heated serving dishes or a serving platter and pour the sauce over them. Serve immediately.

Serves 4
Preparation time: *15–20 minutes*
Cooking time: *25–35 minutes*

Beef Olives

stuffed with cheese, ham, and basil

This is both elegant and simple — and makes a perfect entrée for a dinner with company.

2 pounds flank steak
½ cup pecorino cheese, grated
2 slices raw ham (prosciutto crudo), chopped
3 garlic cloves, crushed
3 tablespoons chopped fresh parsley
1 tablespoon chopped fresh basil
3 tablespoons olive oil
salt and freshly ground black pepper

Tomato sauce
1 onion, chopped
2 garlic cloves, crushed
2 pounds tomatoes, skinned (see page 20)
and chopped
1 tablespoon tomato paste
½ cup red wine
salt and freshly ground black pepper

cut the beef into thin slices and place between 2 sheets of parchment or nonstick baking paper. Flatten the slices of beef with a rolling pin and then season with salt and pepper.

make the stuffing: put the grated pecorino cheese in a bowl with the chopped ham, garlic, parsley, and basil.

mix together well and spread a little of this mixture on each piece of beef. Roll up, folding in the sides, and tie securely with thread or thin string.

heat the olive oil in a large saucepan and gently fry the beef olives until they are slightly brown all over, turning as necessary. Remove from the pan and keep warm.

make the sauce: add the onion and garlic to the oil in the pan and sauté until soft. Add the tomatoes, tomato paste, wine and seasoning. Bring to a boil and then add the beef olives..

cover and simmer gently for 1½–2 hours or until tender. Remove the string from the beef olives and serve them hot. Serve the sauce separately.

Serves 6
Preparation time: *20 minutes*
Cooking time: *1½–2¼ hours*

Braised Beef
in red wine with rosemary

The long, slow cooking method in this recipe is an ideal way to bring out the flavors of any piece of beef suitable for braising.

3 pound cut of beef – chuck or flank, rolled
1 onion, sliced
1 carrot, sliced
1 celery stick, sliced
2 garlic cloves, crushed
2 bay leaves
6 peppercorns
2½ cups red wine such as Barolo
2 tablespoons bacon fat or lard
1 onion, finely chopped
1 sprig of rosemary
salt and freshly ground pepper

put the meat in a deep bowl. Add the sliced onion, carrot, celery, garlic, bay leaves, peppercorns and red wine. Cover the bowl and place in the refrigerator to marinate for 24 hours, turning the beef several times. Lift the meat out of the marinade and dry it carefully. Reserve the marinade.

heat the bacon fat or drippings in a large flameproof casserole and sauté the chopped onion over low heat for about 5 minutes or until it is soft and golden. Add the beef, increase the heat, and brown quickly on all sides.

strain the reserved marinade into the casserole and bring to a boil. Add the rosemary sprig and season with salt and pepper.

lower the heat, cover tightly and simmer very gently for at least 3 hours or until the meat is tender. Turn the meat once halfway through cooking.

transfer the meat to a carving dish or board and slice fairly thickly. Arrange the slices on a warm serving dish. If the sauce is too thin, reduce a little by rapid boiling.

remove the rosemary and pour the sauce over the meat. Serve immediately with puréed potatoes and carrots.

Serves 6
Preparation time: *5 minutes, plus 24 hours marinating time*
Cooking time: *3¼ hours*

Mountain Lamb
in wine and mushrooms

Shepherds in the mountains of Basilicata tend their flocks of sheep as they have done for hundreds of years. This is a traditional way of cooking lamb, using fresh mushrooms from the meadows.

3 tablespoons olive oil

2 pounds boned shoulder or leg of lamb, cut into serving pieces (see clipboard below)

4 cups mushrooms,

½ cup dry white wine

salt and freshly ground black pepper

heat the oil in a flameproof casserole, add the meat, and sauté over moderate heat until browned on all sides.

add the mushrooms, wine, and enough water to just cover the meat. Season with salt and pepper to taste.

cover and cook in a preheated moderately hot oven at 375°F for 1 hour or until the meat is tender, stirring occasionally.

serve hot, with steamed spinach and slices of polenta, if desired.

Serves 4
Preparation time: *10 minutes*
Cooking time: *1 hour 15 minutes*
Oven temperature: *375°F*

clipboard: This is a good way to use an economical joint like shoulder of lamb. Buy the leanest piece you can find, however, as it is rather fatty. Your butcher will remove the bone on request.

Braised Lamb
with celery and pearl onions

This is another delicious recipe for mountain lamb, here braised with fresh celery and onions, keeping the flavor of the meat pure and simple.

3 tablespoons olive oil
2 celery sticks, chopped
24 pearl onions, peeled
2 pounds boned leg or shoulder of lamb, cut into serving pieces
2–3 rosemary sprigs, cut into pieces
2 bay leaves
2 cups Chicken Broth (see page 11)
salt and freshly ground black pepper

heat the oil in a flameproof casserole, add the celery and onions, and fry gently for 5 minutes.

add the meat, half the rosemary, the bay leaves, salt, and pepper to taste. Fry over moderate heat until the meat is browned on all sides.

stir in the broth and just enough water to cover the meat.

cover and simmer for 1 hour or until the meat is tender. Discard the herbs before serving.

serve hot, garnished with the remaining rosemary.

Serves 4
Preparation time: *20 minutes*
Cooking time: *1½ hours*

Sardinian Lamb
with fennel and tomatoes

*Large flocks of sheep graze the high mountains
on the island of Sardinia, where lamb is very plentiful.
This recipe has fennel as a main ingredient,
which gives a pungent, aromatic flavor to the sauce.*

5 tablespoons olive oil
2 pounds boned leg of lamb, cut into serving pieces
1 onion, peeled and chopped
1¾ cups tomatoes, skinned (see page 20) and mashed
6 fennel bulbs, quartered
salt and freshly ground black pepper

heat the oil in a flameproof casserole, add the meat, and fry over moderate heat until lightly browned on all sides.

stir in the onion and fry for an additional 5 minutes. Add the tomatoes and salt and pepper to taste.

lower the heat, cover, and simmer for 40 minutes, adding a little water if the casserole becomes too dry during cooking.

meanwhile, cook the fennel in boiling salted water for 20 minutes. Drain and reserve 1 cup of the cooking liquid.

add the fennel and the reserved cooking liquid to the casserole, and continue cooking for about 20 minutes until the meat is tender. The casserole should be fairly dry. Serve hot, sprinkled with black pepper.

Serves 4
Preparation time: *20 minutes*
Cooking time: *1–1½ hours*

Scallopine alla Milanese

Veal is extremely popular in Italy, and is a traditional favorite on every Italian restaurant menu. This recipe is easy and quick to cook at home.

4 veal scallops, each weighing 4 ounces
1–2 eggs, beaten
dry bread crumbs for coating
6 tablespoons butter
salt and freshly ground black pepper

Garnish
lemon twists
parsley sprigs, chopped

beat the veal lightly with a mallet to flatten.

dip into the beaten egg and coat with bread crumbs.

melt the butter in a large skillet and fry the veal for 2–3 minutes on each side, until tender and golden brown.

transfer the cooked veal to a warmed serving dish and sprinkle with salt and pepper to taste.

garnish with lemon twists and chopped parsley and serve immediately with fresh green beans.

Serves 4
Preparation time: *10 minutes*
Cooking time: *8–10 minutes*

Scallopine alla Bolognese

The Bolognese style of cooking veal scallops adds the rich, melting flavors of marsala wine, cheese, and Parma ham to the delicate meat.

8 small veal scallops, weighing about 3 ounces each
flour for coating
6 tablespoons butter
8 thin slices Parma ham
8 thin slices Swiss cheese
3 tablespoons Marsala
3 tablespoons Chicken Broth (see page 11)
salt and freshly ground black pepper

beat the scallops lightly with a rolling pin to thin them out. Sprinkle each one with a little salt and coat them with flour.

melt the butter in a large skillet, and when foaming, sauté the scallops for about 6–8 minutes on both sides until they are browned and cooked. Arrange them side-by-side in a buttered ovenproof dish.

cover each scallop with a slice of ham and then top with a slice of cheese. Leave in a warm place while you deglaze the pan.

add the Marsala and broth to the buttery juices in the pan and season with pepper. Bring to a boil, scraping the bottom of the pan with a wooden spoon and stirring well. Spoon the sauce around the scallops in the ovenproof dish and season with pepper. Place in a preheated oven at 450°F, or under the broiler for 5–10 minutes until the cheese has melted. Add a few grinds of black pepper and serve hot.

Serves 4
Preparation time: *10 minutes*
Cooking time: *14–20 minutes*
Oven temperature: *450°F*

Veal Scallops

and sage with Parma ham

This dish, which appears on restaurant menus as Saltimbocca alla Romana, and is a perfect example of the Italian genius for combining ingredients which make a happy marriage of flavor and texture.

8 small veal slices, weighing about 2 ounces each
8 paper thin slices of Parma ham
8 fresh sage leaves
6 tablespoons butter
6 tablespoons Marsala or dry white wine
salt
fresh sage leaves, to garnish

beat the scallops out thinly and trim the slices of ham to about the same size as the scallops.

sprinkle each scallop with a pinch of salt and place a sage leaf on top. Cover each scallop with a slice of ham and secure with a toothpick soaked previously in cold water. Do not roll them up.

heat 4 tablespoons of the butter in a large skillet. When the butter foams, add the scallops, and sauté briskly on both sides, removing the cocktail stick before turning. Cook until golden – about 6–8 minutes. Remove from the pan and keep warm.

add the Marsala or white wine to the buttery juices left in the pan. Bring to a boil, scraping the bottom of the pan with a wooden spoon and stirring well. Stir in the remaining butter and spoon the sauce over the scallops. Garnish with fresh sage leaves.

Serves 4
Preparation time: *10 minutes*
Cooking time: *12–15 minutes*

Milanese Veal
stuffed with prosciutto and Parmesan

This is a clever way of making the meat go further, while adding extra flavors.

12 small thin slices of veal
6 short wooden skewers
6 fresh sage leaves
2 slices bacon
4 tablespoons butter
4 tablespoons Marsala
4 tablespoons dry white wine
3 fresh sage leaves, roughly chopped

Filling

2 ounces raw smoked ham (prosciutto crudo),
chopped
1 chicken liver, finely chopped
2 tablespoons fresh white bread crumbs
2 tablespoons freshly grated Parmesan cheese
1 teaspoon minced parsley
1 egg, beaten
¼ teaspoon freshly grated nutmeg
salt and freshly ground black pepper

make the filling: put the chopped ham, chicken liver, bread crumbs, Parmesan, and parsley in a bowl. Bind together with the beaten egg and season to taste with nutmeg, salt, and pepper.

beat the slices of veal flat with a rolling pin. Put some of the filling on each slice of veal and roll it up. Thread 2 veal rolls on to each of 6 short wooden skewers soaked previously in cold water, together with a sage leaf. Cut each bacon slice into 3 pieces and then thread one on to each skewer.

heat the butter in a skillet and then sauté the veal rolls until they are evenly cooked and golden brown, turning occasionally. Remove the veal rolls from the pan and keep warm while you make the sauce.

add the Marsala and wine to the buttery pan juices and bring to a boil, scraping the bottom of the pan clean with a wooden spoon. Add the chopped sage and simmer for 3–5 minutes until reduced slightly. Pour the sauce over the veal rolls and serve immediately.

Serves 4–6
Preparation time: *15 minutes*
Cooking time: *12–15 minutes*

Salamelle Sausage
with broccoli and garlic

The hearty flavors of deliciously spicy, pungent salamelle sausages make a perfect match with the robust taste of fresh green broccoli.

2 tablespoons shortening or lard
2 garlic cloves, chopped
1 piece of canned pimiento
1 pound salamelle or Italian-style sausage links
6 cups broccoli flowerets
salt and freshly ground black pepper

melt the shortening or lard in a flameproof casserole, add the garlic, and fry gently until browned.

stir in the pimiento, sausages and salt and pepper to taste.

cover and bake in a preheated moderate oven at 375°F for about 45 minutes until the sausages are cooked.

meanwhile, cook the broccoli in boiling salted water for 15 minutes until tender. Drain and place in a warmed serving dish.

add the sausages, toss well, and serve immediately.

Serves 4
Preparation time: *5–10 minutes*
Cooking time: *1 hour*
Oven temperature: *375°F*

clipboard: *Salamelle* is a traditional Italian cooking sausage, sold in small links, and is available from Italian food stores or at supermarket delicatessen counters. It is made in several varieties, some of which are hot and peppery.

Calves' Liver
cooked Venetian-style

This is the speciality of one of Italy's most beautiful cities. The delicate combination of wafer-thin, prime meat with onions and parsley is a world away from "liver and onions."

3–4 tablespoons olive oil
2 tablespoons butter
4 medium onions, sliced
I tablespoon minced parsley, plus extra to garnish
I pound calves' liver, sliced very thinly
4 tablespoons Beef Broth (see page 10)
salt and freshly ground black pepper
flat-leaved parsley, to garnish

heat the oil and butter in a skillet, add the onions and parsley, and cook gently for 2–3 minutes.

add the liver, increase the heat, and stir in the broth.

cook the liver for 5 minutes, then remove from the heat and add salt and pepper to taste.

serve immediately on a bed of mashed potatoes, topped with sautéed mushrooms, and garnished with chopped parsley.

Serves 4
Preparation time: *5 minutes*
Cooking time: *10–15 minutes*

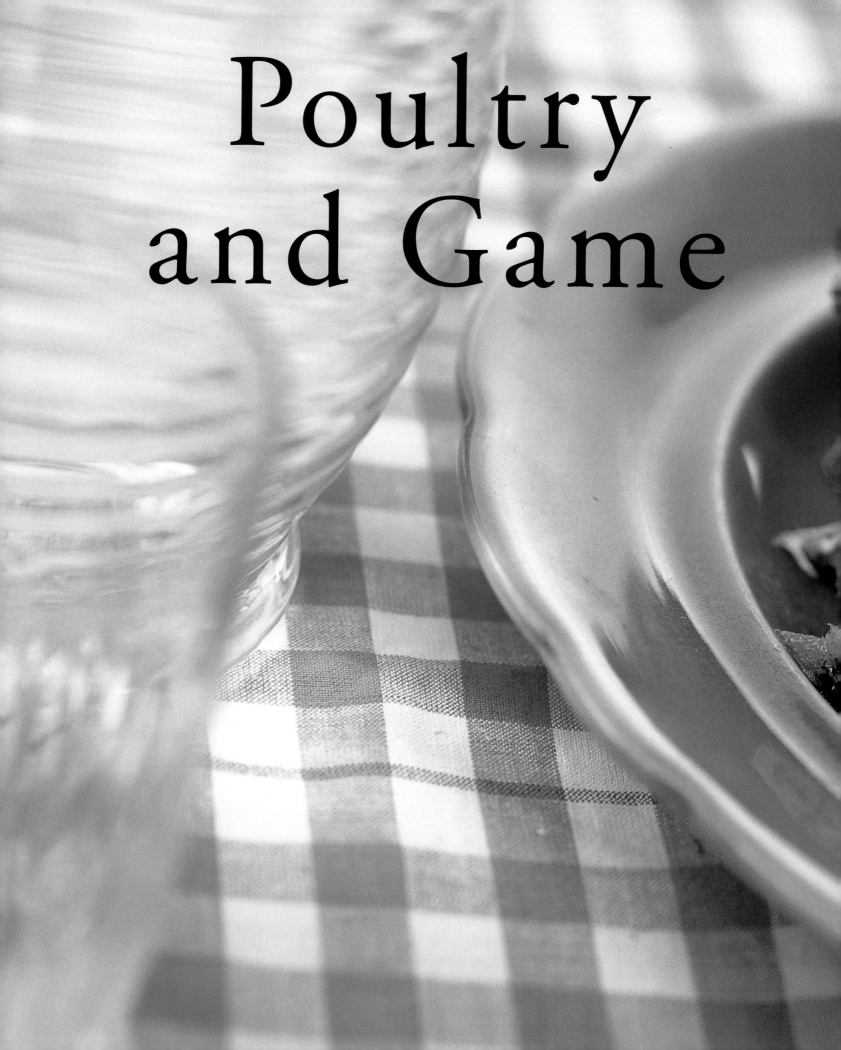

Poultry
and Game

Chicken Marengo

Shrimp, eggs, and fried croûtons give this braised chicken dish extra substance and flavor

8–10 tablespoons olive oil

1 x 3 pound chicken, jointed

4 ripe tomatoes, skinned (see page 20) seeded, and chopped

2 garlic cloves, crushed

1¼ cups dry white wine

2 x ¼ inch slices of bread, crusts removed and cut into triangles

4–6 jumbo shrimp

4–6 eggs

salt and freshly ground black pepper

2 tablespoons chopped parsley, to garnish

heat 2–3 tablespoons of oil in a flameproof casserole and fry the chicken pieces until golden brown on all sides. Remove from the pan. Pour some of the oil from the pan, if necessary, and add the tomatoes, garlic, and white wine. Season to taste and mix well.

return the chicken to the pan, bring to a boil, and bake in a preheated oven at 375°F for 35–45 minutes or until it is tender.

meanwhile, heat another 2–3 tablespoons of oil in a skillet and fry the bread until golden brown on all sides. Remove from the pan and keep hot. Fry the shrimp for 2–3 minutes until cooked through. Keep hot. Heat another 2–3 tablespoons of olive oil in a clean pan and fry the eggs.

when the chicken is cooked, arrange it on a hot serving dish. If necessary, boil the sauce to reduce it to a thin coating consistency. Check the seasoning and pour over the chicken.

arrange the shrimp, eggs, and fried croûtons around the sides of the dish. Sprinkle with parsley before serving. Serve hot.

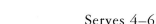

Serves 4–6
Preparation time: *30–40 minutes*
Cooking time: *50–55 minutes*
Oven temperature: *375°F*

clipboard: This dish is based on one created by Napoleon's chef after the Battle of Marengo using what ingredients he could find near the battlefield. To emulate the deep-fried eggs of the original recipe, fry the eggs on both sides.

Pollo alla Cacciatore

This is typical "hunter-style" cooking which gives the chicken a hearty, country flavor.

4 tablespoons olive oil

4 slices pancetta or unsmoked bacon, chopped

1 large chicken (about 3 pounds), cut into 4 portions

2 garlic cloves, crushed

2 red onions, roughly chopped

4 tomatoes, skinned (see page 20) and chopped

2 cups sliced mushrooms

1 sprig of rosemary

1 bay leaf

⅔ cup dry white wine

1¼ cups Chicken Broth (see page 111)

salt and freshly ground black pepper

1 tablespoon chopped parsley, to garnish

heat the oil in a large skillet and fry the pancetta or bacon for 2–3 minutes until browned.

stir occasionally to prevent the pancetta or bacon from sticking. Remove and keep warm.

put the chicken portions in the pan and sauté in the oil, turning occasionally, until they are golden brown all over.

remove the chicken from the pan and keep warm. Add the garlic, onions, tomatoes, and mushrooms and cook gently over low heat for 5 minutes, stirring occasionally. Return the chicken to the skillet.

add the herbs, then pour in the wine and chicken broth. Simmer gently for about 1 hour until the chicken is tender and the sauce reduced. Season to taste with salt and pepper.

Serves 4
Preparation time: *15 minutes*
Cooking time: *1¼ hours*

Pan-fried chicken

A quick and simple dish that relies on the quality of its ingredients. Serve it with a tossed green salad or a fresh green vegetable such as snowpeas, French beans ,or broccoli.

3 tablespoons olive oil
I tablespoon butter
4 chicken breasts, skinned
¾ cup dry white wine
4-6 fresh sage leaves, roughly chopped
3 tablespoons balsamic or sherry vinegar
salt and freshly ground black pepper
fresh sage leaves, to garnish

heat the oil and butter in a large non-stick skillet until foaming. Add the chicken and cook over low to moderate heat for 5-7 minutes until golden brown on both sides, turning once.

pour the wine over the chicken and sprinkle over the chopped sage and salt and pepper to taste. Cover and cook over low heat for 15 minutes, spooning the sauce over the chicken from time to time and turning the chicken halfway through cooking.

remove the chicken to warmed dinner plates and keep warm. Add the vinegar to the pan juices, increase the heat to high, and stir until the juices are reduced. Spoon the juices over the chicken, garnish with sage leaves, and serve immediately.

Serves 4
Preparation time: *5 minutes*
Cooking time: *25–30 minutes*

clipboard: Chicken breasts on the bone have the most tender, moist meat, and they are less likely to dry out during cooking. Boneless chicken breasts are easier to obtain and they can be used for this dish, but take care to baste them frequently and not to overcook them — the total cooking time should be only 15 minutes.

Game Hens
spatchcocked and barbecued

2 Rock Cornish game hens, spatchcocked, (see clipboard)
½ cup olive oil
6 tablespoons lemon juice
2 tablespoons mixed peppercorns, crushed coarsely in a mortar with a pestle
kosher salt or rock salt
lemon wedges, to serve

put the game hens in a non-metallic dish, and slash them all over with the point of a small sharp knife.

whisk together the oil, lemon juice, and crushed peppercorns, and brush all over the game hens, working the marinade into the cuts in the meat. Cover and leave to marinate for at least 4 hours, preferably overnight in the refrigerator.

prepare the barbecue and let it burn until the flames have died down and the coals have turned gray. Sprinkle the skin side of the game hens with salt, then place them skin-side down on the barbecue grill. Cook for 15 minutes, then turn the game hens over and cook for an additional 10 minutes.

remove the game hens from the barbecue grill and cut each bird in half lengthwise with poultry shears. Serve hot, warm or cold, with lemon wedges for squeezing.

Serves 4
Preparation time: *10 minutes*, plus marinating
Cooking time: *25 minutes*

clipboard: Spatchcocking is simple: with the bird breast-side down, cut along each side of the backbone with poultry shears. Discard the backbone, or use in the stockpot. Put the bird breast-side up on a board and press hard with the heels of your hand on the breastbone to break it. To keep the bird flat during cooking, push 2 metal skewers through the bird, one through the wings with the breast in between, the other through the thighs.

Wild Boar
with sausage and polenta

For the Marinade

3 cups red wine
1 onion, roughly chopped
1 carrot, roughly chopped
1 celery stick, roughly chopped
1 bay leaf
1 sprig each of sage and rosemary
1 tablespoon crushed black peppercorns
1 tablespoon crushed juniper berries

3 pounds boneless wild boar, cut into large cubes
6 tablespoons olive oil
1 onion, minced
1 carrot, finely chopped
1 celery stick, finely chopped
1 garlic clove, crushed
2 salamelle sausage links cut into chunks
2½ cups Beef Broth (see page 10)
1¼ cups red wine
½ cup passata (strained fresh tomato pulp)
2 tablespoons chopped flat-leaved parsley
1 teaspoon chopped fresh sage
1 teaspoon chopped fresh thyme
salt and freshly ground black pepper
fresh sage leaves, to garnish

For the polenta

3 cups water
1 cup milk
1 cup quick-cook polenta
4 tablespoons butter
1 teaspoon salt

start by making the marinade for the meat. Put all the ingredients for the marinade in a saucepan and bring to a boil. Pour into a large bowl, leave to cool, then add the meat. Cover and marinate in the refrigerator overnight. The next day, remove the meat from the marinade with a slotted spoon and pat dry with paper towel. Discard the marinade.

heat the oil in a flameproof casserole, add the onion, carrot, celery and garlic and cook gently, stirring frequently, for about 5 minutes until softened but not colored.

add the meat and sausages and cook over a medium heat, stirring, until browned on all sides, then add the stock, wine and passata and bring to a boil. Lower the heat and add the herbs and salt and pepper to taste, cover and simmer very gently for 2 hours or until the meat is tender.

cook the polenta: bring the water to the boil in a large heavy saucepan, add 1 teaspoon salt, then sprinkle in the polenta in a thin, steady stream, stirring all the time with a wooden spoon. Cook over a low heat, stirring constantly, for 8 minutes or according to the packet instructions. Remove from the heat and beat in the butter until melted.

divide the polenta between 4 warmed dinner plates, then spoon the stew over and around. Garnish with sage leaves and serve immediately.

Serves 4
Preparation time: *30 minutes*, plus marinating
Cooking time: *2–2½ hours*

clipboard: If wild boar is not available, use venison or buffalo.

Chicken
with tomatoes and pimiento

Colorful, warming, and easy-to-prepare, this dish could be served with boiled potatoes and a mixed salad.

3–4 tablespoons olive oil
I small onion, sliced
2 garlic cloves, crushed
I x 2½ pound oven-ready chicken, cut into serving pieces
I small piece canned pimiento, chopped
4 medium tomatoes
I tablespoon tomato paste
3–4 tablespoons dry white wine
few rosemary sprigs
6–8 tablespoons Chicken Broth (see page 11)
salt and freshly ground black pepper

heat the oil in a flameproof casserole, add the onion and garlic and fry gently for 15 minutes.

add the chicken pieces with the pimiento, tomatoes, salt and pepper to taste, and fry, turning, over moderate heat until evenly browned on all sides.

mix the tomato paste with a little lukewarm water, then stir into the casserole with the wine.

reduce the heat, cover, and continue cooking gently for 30 minutes.

chop one of the rosemary sprigs and sprinkle over the chicken.

cook for an additional 30 minutes or until the chicken is tender, adding a little of the broth occasionally to moisten.

serve hot, garnished with the remaining rosemary.

Serves 4
Preparation time: *20–30 minutes*
Cooking time: *1½ hours*

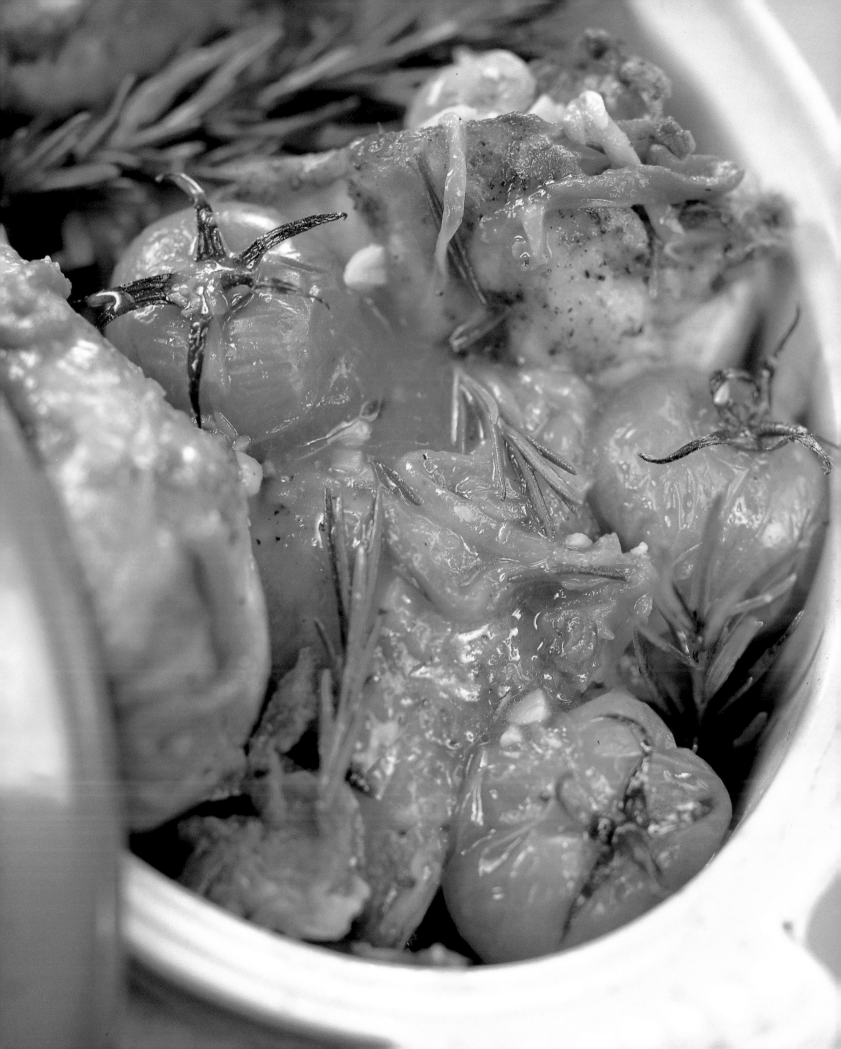

Roast Chicken
with egg and cheese stuffing

*A triumph of Italian taste and invention,
this is a refreshingly different way
of cooking roast chicken.*

2 tablespoons butter
1 x 3-pound oven-ready chicken with giblets
1¼ cups dry bread crumbs
3 tomatoes, skinned (see page 20) and chopped
1 egg, beaten
½ cup grated pecorino cheese
7 tablespoons milk
4 tablespoons light cream
1 hard-boiled egg
4 tablespoons olive oil
salt and freshly ground black pepper

melt the butter in a heavy-based skillet, chop the chicken giblets and add to the pan. Fry gently for 10 minutes.

add the bread crumbs and fry until browned, then add the tomatoes and simmer for 10 minutes. Remove from the heat and leave to cool.

add the egg to the mixture with the cheese, milk, cream, and salt and pepper to taste.

mix thoroughly. Stuff the chicken with this mixture, putting the hard-boiled egg in the center. Sew the opening securely with trussing thread or clean string.

place the chicken in an oiled roasting pan, pour the olive oil over it, and sprinkle with salt and pepper to taste.

roast in a preheated, moderately hot oven at 400°F for 1½ hours or until the chicken is tender. Serve immediately.

Serves 6
Preparation time: *30 minutes*
Cooking time: *1½-2 hours*
Oven temperature: *400°F*

Guinea Fowl

This bird, which is related to the pheasant, was once hunted as game but has long been reared domestically. Its flesh has a distinctive flavor and can be roasted or casseroled.

1 x 3–3½ pound guinea fowl, jointed
(see clipboard)
4 tablespoons butter
2–3 tablespoons olive oil
4 tomatoes, skinned (see page 20), seeded and sliced
or 1¾ cups canned tomatoes, drained,
seeded, and sliced
salt and pepper
1 tablespoon minced parsley, to garnish

season the guinea fowl with salt and pepper. Heat the butter and oil in a flameproof casserole and brown the pieces of guinea fowl well on all sides over a good heat.

lower the heat, cover with a tight-fitting lid and cook over a gentle heat, turning the pieces of guinea fowl from time to time for 25–35 minutes or until the bird is tender.

drain off most of the fat from the pan and add the tomatoes. Cook until they thicken slightly and season to taste. Pour into a serving dish, sprinkle over the parsley and serve hot with small roast potatoes.

Serves 4
Preparation time: *15–20 minutes*
Cooking time: *40–45 minutes*

clipboard: To joint the guinea fowl, place it on a board, breast uppermost, and cut through the skin between the body and the leg. Press the whole leg (the thigh and drumstick) outward to break the joint. Cut through any flesh, sinew or skin holding the leg to the carcass. Cut through the joint between the thigh and the drumstick. Repeat on the other side. Trim the first two joints away from the wing. Cut the breast away from the wing and break the wing joint in the same way as the leg. Cut through this joint. Cut the breast into two pieces.

Turkey Breasts
with Parmesan, egg, and spinach

2 eggs
4 tablespoons grated Parmesan cheese
3–4 tablespoons olive oil
2½ cups chopped spinach
pinch of nutmeg
4 slices lean rindless bacon
2 x 8–10 ounces turkey breast fillets
2 tablespoons butter
1¼ cups dry white wine
½ teaspoon chopped rosemary
salt and freshly ground black pepper

whisk one of the eggs with half the Parmesan and season well. Heat a scant tablespoon of oil in a 6 inch skillet. Cook until golden brown, then turn over and cook on the reverse side. Make another omelet.

heat a tablespoon of oil in another pan, and cook the spinach over a moderate heat until it softens. Season with nutmeg, salt, and pepper.

place an omelet, half the spinach, and 2 slices of bacon on each prepared turkey fillet, Roll up toward the pointed end and secure with toothpicks, previously soaked in cold water, and string.

melt the butter and a tablespoon of oil in a flameproof casserole and brown the turkey on all sides. Pour on the wine, add the rosemary, season, cover, and cook in a preheated oven at 350°F for 1–1¼ hours until the turkey is tender. Take the turkey fillets from the pan and remove the toothpicks and strings. Cut into thick slices and arrange on a dish. Pour over the cooking liquid and serve hot with fresh, steamed spinach.

Serves 4–6
Preparation Time: *40–45 minutes*
Cooking Time: *1¼–1½ hours*
Oven temperature: *350°F*

clipboard: To prepare turkey fillets, place them on a board. Hold a small knife parallel to the board and make a cut right through the thickest side. Cut almost through to the other edge right down the length of the fillet, then open it out and flatten it well. Remove the white sinew, which is clearly visible, with the point of a knife.

Roast Turkey
with juniper and pomegranates

1 x 4 pound oven ready turkey with giblets
4 tablespoons butter, diced
⅔ cup olive oil
4 juniper berries
2 rosemary sprigs, (1 to garnish)
1 cup dry white wine
2 pomegranates
juice of ½ lemon
4 tablespoons Chicken Broth (see page 11)
salt and freshly ground black pepper

sprinkle the turkey inside and out with salt, then place one-third of the butter in the cavity. Sew the opening with trussing thread or string. Place the turkey in an oiled roasting pan.

top with the remaining butter, 7 tablespoons of oil, the juniper berries, and rosemary, then add the wine. Roast in a preheated moderate oven at 350°F for 1½ hours, basting the turkey occasionally with the wine and cooking juices.

add the juice of 1 pomegranate and cook for an additional 1 hour or until the turkey is almost tender.

meanwhile, chop the turkey liver and gizzard finely. Heat the remaining oil in a heavy pan, add the liver and gizzard, and fry until browned. Remove from the heat and set aside.

add the juice of another pomegranate and salt and pepper to taste to the turkey. Roast for an additional 10 minutes, then remove the turkey from the pan, and cut into serving pieces. Arrange in an ovenproof serving dish.

skim off the fat from the cooking juices and place the pan over moderate heat. Add the lemon juice and broth and boil until reduced by about half. Strain and stir into the giblet mixture. Pour this sauce over the turkey pieces and return to the oven for an additional 7–8 minutes. Serve immediately, garnished with a sprig of fresh rosemary..

Serves 8
Preparation time: *30 minutes*
Cooking time: *2 hours 50 minutes*
Oven temperature: *350°F*

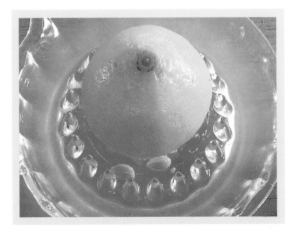

Braised Pheasant

with savory risotto

Italians are very fond of game. This is one of many excellent recipes for pheasant and other game.

1 x 2½ pound pheasant, cleaned
salt
4 slices bacon, derinded
4 tablespoons olive oil
1 onion, chopped
1 carrot, chopped
1 celery stick, chopped
1 bay leaf
⅔ cup Chicken Broth (see page 11)

Risotto
4 tablespoons butter
1 small onion, chopped
2 tablespoons Arborio rice
3–4 tablespoons dry white wine
1 quart hot Chicken Broth (see page 11)
4 tablespoons Parmesan cheese, grated
freshly ground black pepper

sprinkle the pheasant inside and out with salt, then wrap the bacon around the outside and secure with string.

heat the oil in a flameproof casserole, add the chopped vegetables and the bay leaf and fry gently until lightly colored. Add the pheasant and fry until browned on all sides, then lower the heat, cover and cook gently for 40 minutes until the pheasant is tender, adding a little broth from time to time to prevent sticking.

meanwhile, make the risotto. Melt the butter in a heavy pan, add the onion and cook gently for 5 minutes. Add the rice and stir for 2–3 minutes over moderate heat, then add the wine and boil until reduced, stirring constantly. Continue cooking for 20 minutes, adding the broth a cupful at a time, as the liquid is absorbed.

remove from the heat, stir in the Parmesan and salt and pepper to taste, then turn into a warmed serving dish. Remove the pheasant from the casserole and place on top of the risotto. Spoon over the cooking liquid. Serve immediately.

Serves 4–6
Preparation time: *30 minutes*
Cooking time: *1 hour 10 minutes*

Wild Rabbit
braised with red wine and olives

*Wild rabbit has wonderful, herb-scented flesh,
and this recipe brings out its flavor to perfection.*

7 tablespoons olive oil
1 x 2½ pound wild rabbit, cut into serving pieces
2 garlic cloves, chopped
1 rosemary sprig, chopped
1 cup red wine
6–8 tablespoons Chicken Broth (see page 11)
2 tomatoes, skinned (see page 20) and mashed
1 cup black olives, halved and pitted
salt and freshly ground black pepper

heat the oil in a flameproof casserole, add the rabbit, and sprinkle with the garlic and rosemary.

fry gently until the rabbit is browned on all sides, turning frequently.

add the wine and salt, and pepper to taste. Cover and simmer for 30 minutes, adding a little broth to moisten as necessary.

add the tomatoes and olives and cook for an additional 40 minutes until the rabbit is tender. Serve hot on a bed of tagliatelle.

Serves 4
Preparation time: *10 minutes*
Cooking time: *1¼ hours*

clipboard: Try and get wild rabbit if possible, as the flavor is stronger than the farmed variety. If you are not able to find it, use farmed rabbit — it will still taste very good.

Rabbit Casserole
with fennel and bacon

The smoky flavors of fennel and ham combine beautifully with rabbit. Serve this with pasta and a green salad.

2 fennel bulbs (white part only), quartered

3 garlic cloves, peeled

1 x 2½ pounds rabbit, with liver

4 ounces bacon or raw ham

7 tablespoons olive oil

1 cup fresh bread crumbs, soaked in a little milk and squeezed dry

salt and freshly ground black pepper

fennel slivers, to garnish

cover the fennel and 2 cloves of garlic in boiling salted water and cook for 15 minutes. Drain thoroughly, reserving the cooking liquid, but discarding the garlic. Chop the fennel finely.

mince the liver together with the bacon or raw ham and the remaining garlic. Heat 2 tablespoons oil in a flameproof casserole, add the fennel and liver mixture.

cook gently for 10 minutes, then mix with the bread crumbs and salt and pepper to taste. Stuff the rabbit with this mixture, then sew up the opening with trussing thread or string.

place the rabbit in a roasting pan and sprinkle with the remaining oil and salt and pepper to taste.

cover with foil and roast in a preheated oven at 350°F for 1½ hours or until the rabbit is tender, basting occasionally with the fennel cooking liquid. Transfer the rabbit to a serving platter garnished with fennel. Serve hot.

Serves 4

Preparation time: *15–20 minutes*

Cooking time: *2 hours*

Oven temperature: *350°F*

Hare Casserole

Hare is very strongly flavored, and the aromatic marinade of juniper and peppercorns enhances its taste.

1 medium hare, jointed
1 x quantity marinade (see clipboard below)
4 tablespoons all-purpose flour, seasoned with salt and pepper
4 tablespoons butter
2 tablespoons olive oil
2 tablespoons brandy
salt and pepper

place the pieces of hare in a deep bowl with the vegetables, herbs, spices, red wine, and vinegar of the marinade. Cover and refrigerate for 24–48 hours, turning the hare from time to time in the liquid.

remove the hare from the marinade and drain until dry. Coat the hare with seasoned flour. Heat the butter and oil in a flameproof casserole and brown the hare on all sides.

pour all the marinade into the pan and season to taste with salt. Bring to a boil, cover and cook in a preheated oven at 375°F for about 2 hours, until the hare is tender.

remove the hare from the casserole and place on a hot serving dish. Remove the herbs and spices from the pan and purée the vegetables in the sauce in a food processor or blender. Return to the casserole and adjust the consistency of the sauce and the seasoning if necessary. Add the brandy, bring to a boil, then pour it over the hare, and serve hot with pasta.

Serves 4–6
Preparation time: *30–40 minutes, plus marinating*
Cooking time: 2¼–2¾ hours
Oven temperature: *375°F*

clipboard: Marinades tenderize game and meat and give extra flavor. This is a typical recipe: 1 carrot, celery stick, and large onion, all neatly sliced, 1–2 garlic cloves, crushed, 6–8 parsley stalks, 1 sprig thyme or rosemary, 2 bay leaves, 4 juniper berries, 8 peppercorns, 2½ cups red wine.

Venison *with brandy and red currant sauce*

1¼–1½ pound cut of venison, diced
1 quantity marinade (see page 164)
2 tablespoons olive oil
4 slices rindless streaky bacon, diced
2–3 tablespoons seasoned flour
6–8 tablespoons red currant jelly
2 tablespoons grappa or brandy
salt and pepper

place the venison and marinade in a bowl, cover, and refrigerate for at least 24 hours, turning the venison from time to time. Remove the meat from the marinade and drain until dry.

heat the oil in a pan and cook the bacon until golden brown. Remove from the pan. Toss the venison in the seasoned flour and brown it on all sides in the hot oil.

add the bacon and the marinade. Season lightly, cover and simmer gently on top of the stove, or cook in a preheated oven at 350°F for 1½–2 hours.

remove the venison from the pan, cover, and keep hot. Strain the cooking liquid into a clean pan and whisk in 2 tablespoons of red currant jelly. Boil until the sauce reduces to a thin coating consistency. Pour over the meat and keep hot.

melt the remaining red currant jelly in a pan and whisk until smooth. Add the grappa or brandy and boil for about one minute. Pour into a sauce boat and serve separately.

Serves 4–6
Preparation time: *30–35 minutes, plus 24 hours marinating*
Cooking time: *1½–2½ hours*
Oven temperature: *350°F*

clipboard: For this dish, casserole or shoulder venison is ideal. It is quite reasonable to buy, the price being comparable with other braising meats. Venison is a very lean meat.

Pizza, Rice, and Polenta

Basic Dough
for home-made pizza

It is so useful to be able to make your own pizza from scratch, and this recipe gives excellent results.

2 tablespoons fresh yeast
1¼ cups lukewarm water
1 cup all-purpose flour, plus extra for
working the dough
1 teaspoon salt

blend the yeast with a little of the lukewarm water. Sift the flour and salt into a large mixing bowl.

make a well in the center and pour in the yeast mixture and the remaining lukewarm water. Using your hand and with a circular movement, gradually work the flour into the liquid, moving from the center of the well outward to form a sticky, elastic dough.

turn out the dough on to a floured work surface and knead it well, adding more flour if necessary, until it stops sticking to your knuckles and the work surface. Knead for approximately 10 minutes until it is smooth and elastic. At this stage, if you are making more than one pizza, divide the dough into the required number of pieces and knead each one into a ball.

sprinkle the bottom of the mixing bowl with flour and leave the dough to rise, covering the bowl with a damp cloth, for approximately 1 hour. The time required will depend upon the warmth of the kitchen. The dough is ready for rolling out when it has doubled in size.

Serves 4: makes 2 large, 4 small pizzas
Preparation time: *10 minutes, plus kneading and rising*

clipboard: This amount of dough can be shaped into two large round pizzas, approximately 12 inches in diameter, one large rectangular pizza, or four individual pizzas approximately 8 inches in diameter. Pizza pans will help you shape the pizza better than simple baking trays or cookie sheets. The dough must be spread thinly, to about ¼ inch thick.

Fresh Pizza
with onions and eggs

Pizzas are said to have been invented by frugal Neapolitans as a way to use up bread dough. This recipe shows how you can achieve delicious, authentic results from the simplest of ingredients.

4–5 tablespoons olive oil
5-6 medium onions, finely sliced
½ quantity basic pizza dough (see page 170)
2–3 hard-boiled eggs, sliced
salt and pepper
1–2 tablespoons chopped parsley, to garnish

heat 3–4 tablespoons oil in a pan and cook the onions over moderate heat until they are soft and lightly colored. Season well with salt and pepper.

roll out the dough to 2 x 12 inch circles and place on a cookie sheet. Spread the cooked onions over the surface.

bake in a preheated oven at 450°F for 15–20 minutes until the pizzas are risen and golden brown.

arrange the slices of hard-boiled egg over the top, sprinkle with the remainder of the oil, and return to the oven for an additional 2–3 minutes. Sprinkle chopped parsley over just before serving.

Serves 2
Preparation time: *20 minutes*
Cooking time: *15–20 minutes*
Oven temperature 450°F

clipboard: This pizza recipe can be served hot or cold. If it is to be served cold, do not return it to the oven after the hard-boiled eggs have been arranged on top.

Easter Pizza

Easter is a joyous time in Italy, and many traditional dishes are served then, including this festive pizza

3 eggs
6 tablespoons grated Parmesan cheese
6 tablespoons grated pecorino cheese
1 quantity basic pizza dough, unrisen (see page 170)
olive oil
1¼ cup all-purpose flour
6–8 ounces salami
1–2 hard-boiled eggs, sliced
a little extra olive oil
salt and freshly ground black pepper
pitted black olive, to garnish

beat the eggs and cheeses together, and season with salt. Knead the pizza dough well and press out into a small circle. Pour some of the olive oil and flour into the center. Fold over the edges, press out into a circle again, and repeat the process until all the oil and flour have been incorporated. Knead until smooth.

press out into a larger circle and place the egg mixture in the center. Fold over and knead well until it is incorporated into the dough. Place in an oiled bowl, cover, and keep in a warm place for 1–1½ hours, until doubled in size.

turn out on to a board, knead into a circle and place in a greased 10 inch cake pan. Cover and leave to rise until doubled in size. Bake in a preheated oven at 450°F for 20–30 minutes until it sounds hollow when tapped.

unmold onto a baking tray and return to the oven, upside down, for a few minutes until golden brown. Arrange the salami, hard-boiled eggs, and olive on top. Sprinkle olive oil over the eggs and return to the oven for a few minutes to warm through. Serve immediately, sprinkled with black pepper.

Serves 8–10
Preparation time: *30 minutes, plus rising and proving*
Cooking time: *25–30 minutes*
Oven temperature: *450°F*

clipboard: If this pizza is too large for your requirements, you can make half the quantity and bake it in a 7–8 inch pan. However, you must use the same amount of yeast in the pizza dough as is given for the full quantity.

Saffron Risotto
with sausage and peppers

Fragrant and colorful, this is a luscious risotto.
It should be made with Arborio rice for the best results.

pinch of saffron threads
3 tablespoons olive oil
I small carrot, finely chopped
I red onion, minced
I stick celery, finely chopped
8 ounces Italian sausage, diced
2 fresh sage leaves
2 red and green peppers, cored, seeded
and cut into strips
I¾ cups whole canned tomatoes, drained, seeded
and chopped
I½ cups Arborio rice
4-6 tablespoons grated Parmesan cheese
salt and freshly ground black pepper
sprig fresh sage leaves, to garnish

place the saffron in a small bowl, pour on 2 tablespoons boiling water, and leave until required.

heat the oil and brown the carrot, onion, celery, and sausage. Add the sage and peppers and cook for a few minutes, then add the tomatoes and half the juice from the can. Season and continue to cook for about 30 minutes, adding more juice if necessary, until the vegetables are tender and most of the juice has evaporated.

meanwhile, cook the rice in a large pan of boiling salted water for 12–15 minutes until just tender, then drain well, return to the pan, and stir in the saffron. Mix in well so that all the rice is yellow. If necessary, stir over a gentle heat until the rice is dry.

stir in the vegetable and sausage mix and Parmesan to taste. Pile into an ovenproof dish and cook in a preheated oven at 400°F for 5–10/10–15 minutes until golden brown. Serve hot, garnished with sage.

Serves 4
Preparation time: *20–25 minutes*
Cooking time: *50–60 minutes*
Oven temperature: *400°F*

clipboard: You can buy powdered saffron or whole saffron threads, both of which are used in the same way. If you are unable to obtain saffron, use a little turmeric to color the rice.

Creamy Risotto
with Fontina and Gorgonzola cheese

1½ cups long-grain rice
5 ounces Fontina cheese
5 ounces Gorgonzola cheese
2 cups milk
6 tablespoons butter
3 tablespoons all-purpose flour
¾ cup light cream
salt and pepper

boil the rice in salted water, and drain when just tender.

remove the rind from the Fontina, cut into cubes, and place in a bowl. Cut the Gorgonzola into very small pieces. Put the milk in a small pan over a low heat.

soften two-thirds of the butter in a pan, add the flour, stirring well, then gradually add the hot milk, stirring continuously to make a sauce.

add the small pieces of Gorgonzola gradually, season with a pinch of salt and pepper. Remove from the heat and stir in the cream.

add the drained rice to the bowl with the cubed Fontina and mix with the remaining butter.

make a layer of rice in a buttered ovenproof dish, cover with one-third of the Gorgonzola sauce, add another layer of rice followed by half the remaining Gorgonzola sauce, and repeat for the third time.

place the dish in a moderate oven at 350°F for 10 minutes, then serve immediately. For the best results, the rice needs to be very hot but the sauce on the top should not be brown.

Serves 4
Preparation time: *10 minutes*
Cooking time: *30–40 minutes*
Oven temperature: *350°F*

Polenta
with Fontina cheese

Polenta, a form of cornmeal mush, is one of the basic staples of northern Italian cooking — as basic as potatoes! The yellow cornmeal gives it its distinctive, golden color.

2 quarts water
2 tablespoons fine yellow cornmeal
8 ounces Fontina cheese, diced
4 tablespoons grated Parmesan cheese
⅔ cup butter, melted
salt and freshly ground black pepper

bring the water to the boil in a large pan. Add the polenta gradually in a thin, steady stream, stirring all the time.

add salt and pepper to taste and stir well to mix.

add the Fontina and cook very gently for 8 minutes (or 45 minutes if you are not using quick-cook polenta), stirring frequently.

pour the polenta into a shallow dish and sprinkle with the Parmesan and a little pepper. Pour the melted butter over the top and serve immediately.

Serves 4–6
Preparation time: *10 minutes*
Cooking time: 8 minutes or *45 minutes*

Clipboard: Polenta has to be stirred continuously during cooking to avoid lumps. Buy the instant or quick-cooking type of polenta from an Italian delicatessen or large supermarket. Polenta spits and splutters during cooking, so take care while standing over the pan, and use a long-handled spoon.

Country Risotto
with mixed vegetables

A healthy, fresh-tasting risotto is always welcome. What's more, this recipe can be varied according to what vegetables you have available.

4 tablespoons butter
2 tablespoons olive oil
1 large onion, finely chopped
2 garlic cloves, crushed
½ cup fresh shelled or frozen peas
½ cup small fresh asparagus tips
1 cup small zucchini, sliced
½ cup Arborio rice
4 medium tomatoes, skinned (see page 20), seeded and chopped or 1¾ cups whole tomatoes, drained, seeded and chopped
5 pints Chicken Broth (see page 11)
2–3 tablespoons grated Parmesan cheese
salt and pepper
fresh basil leaves, to garnish

heat the butter and oil in a heavy-based pan and cook the onion and garlic until soft and lightly colored.

add the fresh peas now if using, also the asparagus and zucchini, and cook for 2–3 minutes. Stir in the rice and mix well. Add the tomatoes and the broth a little at a time. Season to taste with salt and pepper.

mix well and cook gently for about 18 minutes, adding more hot broth or water if necessary to keep the rice moist. If you are using frozen peas, add them 5 minutes before the end of the cooking time. When the rice is tender, check the seasoning and stir in the Parmesan to taste.

transfer to a serving dish and sprinkle with the basil just before serving. Serve hot.

Serves 4
Preparation time: *25–30 minutes*
Cooking time: *35–40 minutes*

Clipboard: Any selection of vegetables can be used in this recipe, including green beans, fresh lima beans, sliced mushrooms, or peppers.

Risotto
with wild mushrooms

½ cup butter
1 onion, minced
3 cups wild mushrooms (see clipboard below)
2 cups Arborio rice
5 cups boiling Chicken Broth (see page 11)
⅛ teaspoon powdered saffron or saffron threads
3 tablespoons grated Parmesan cheese,
plus a little extra to serve
salt and freshly ground black pepper

heat half of the butter in a large, heavy-based skillet, add the onion, and fry gently until it is soft and translucent but does not turn color.

add the sliced mushrooms and cook for 2–3 minutes, stirring occasionally. Add the rice and stir over a moderately low heat until all the grains are glistening and beginning to turn translucent around the edges.

stir in ½ cup of boiling broth and simmer very gently until it has been absorbed. Continue adding more broth in this manner until the rice is thoroughly cooked and tender and all the liquid has been absorbed. This will take about 15–20 minutes.

stir in the saffron halfway through cooking. Stir frequently to prevent the rice sticking to the base of the pan, and season with salt and pepper.

when the rice is ready, gently mix in the remaining butter and the Parmesan. The risotto should not be too dry, in fact, it should be quite moist. Serve with extra grated Parmesan.

Serves 4
Preparation time: *5 minutes*
Cooking time: *30 minutes*

Clipboard: Most fresh wild mushrooms will taste good in risotto. Dried dried wild mushrooms are available packaged from supermarkets and Italian delis. They may seem expensive, but they are only used in very small quantities. Before use, put them in a bowl, cover with warm water and leave them to soak for 20–30 minutes.

Seafood Risotto
with mussels and scallops

One of the pleasures of risotto is that you can vary the ingredients — so use whatever fresh shellfish is available in the market.

2 cups fresh mussels in their shells
4 tablespoons olive oil
1 onion, chopped
2 garlic cloves, crushed
1¾ cups Arborio rice
7 cups Fish Broth (see page 11)
½ cup dry white wine
few strands of saffron
1½ cups peeled cooked shrimp
1 cup prepared scallops
1 cup prepared squid
salt and freshly ground black pepper

To garnish
2 tablespoons chopped fresh parsley
sprigs of fresh oregano

prepare the mussels: cover with cold water, and discard any that are cracked or open, or rise to the surface. Scrub well to remove any barnacles, remove the beards, and soak in fresh cold water until ready to cook. Place in a large saucepan with a little water and oil, covered, until they open. Shake the pan occasionally. Drain and set aside, reserving the cooking liquid.

heat the olive oil in a large deep skillet, add the onion and garlic, and fry gently until they are soft and golden, stirring occasionally.

stir in the rice and cook over low heat for 1–2 minutes, stirring until the grains are glistening with oil and almost translucent. Pour in some of the fish broth and the reserved mussel liquid and wine, and bring to a boil.

meanwhile, soak the saffron in a little boiling water and add to the risotto with the prepared prawns, scallops and squid. Reduce the heat to a simmer and cook gently, adding more fish broth as necessary until the rice is tender and creamy and all the liquid has been absorbed. Garnish with chopped parsley and sprigs of oregano.

Serves 4–6
Preparation time: *25 minutes*
Cooking time: *45 minutes*

Chicken Risotto

with white wine and tomatoes

1 x 2-pound oven-ready chicken
2 quarts pints water
2 celery sticks
2 onions
2 carrots
3–4 tablespoons olive oil
7 tablespoons white wine
6 tomatoes, skinned (see page 20)
and mashed
2 cups Arborio rice
6 tablespoons butter, softened
6 tablespoons Parmesan cheese, grated
salt and freshly ground black pepper

remove the bones from the chicken and place them in a large pan with the water. Add 1 celery stick, 1 onion, and 1 carrot, and season liberally with salt and pepper.

bring to a boil, lower the heat, cover and simmer for 1½ hours. Strain the broth and keep hot.

meanwhile dice the chicken meat, removing all the skin. Finely chop the remaining vegetables and fry gently in the olive oil until lightly colored.

add the chicken and fry for an additional 5 minutes, stirring constantly, then add the wine and boil until it evaporates.

add the tomatoes and salt and pepper to taste. Cover and cook gently for 20 minutes, adding a little of the chicken broth if the mixture becomes dry.

stir in the rice, then add 1 cup chicken broth. Cook for 20–25 minutes until the rice is just tender, adding a little more broth to moisten, as necessary.

remove from the heat, add the butter and Parmesan and fold in gently to mix. Serve immediately sprinkled with freshly ground black pepper.

Serves 6
Preparation time: *35 minutes*
Cooking time: *1–2 hours*

Risotto alla Milanese

Melting, creamy, and utterly luxurious, this risotto is justifiably famous all over the world. The finest quality rice is grown south of Milan, and the region is renowned for its superb rice dishes.

⅔ cup butter
½ onion, chopped
7 tablespoons dry white wine
1 quart hot Beef Broth (see page 10)
1¾ cups Arborio rice
¼ teaspoon saffron powder
8 tablespoons grated Parmesan cheese
4 tablespoons light cream
salt and freshly ground black pepper

melt half the butter in a large, heavy-based pan, add the onion and a little pepper and fry gently until golden. Add the wine and 7 tablespoons of the broth. Boil until reduced by half.

add the rice and cook for 5 minutes, stirring constantly, then add the saffron and salt and pepper to taste.

continue cooking for 20 minutes, stirring in the hot broth, a cup at a time, as the liquid is absorbed, until the rice is just tender.

remove from the heat, stir in the remaining butter, the Parmesan and cream and leave to stand for 1 minute. Sprinkle with freshly ground black pepper and serve.

Serves 4–6
Preparation time: *10 minutes*
Cooking time: *35 minutes*

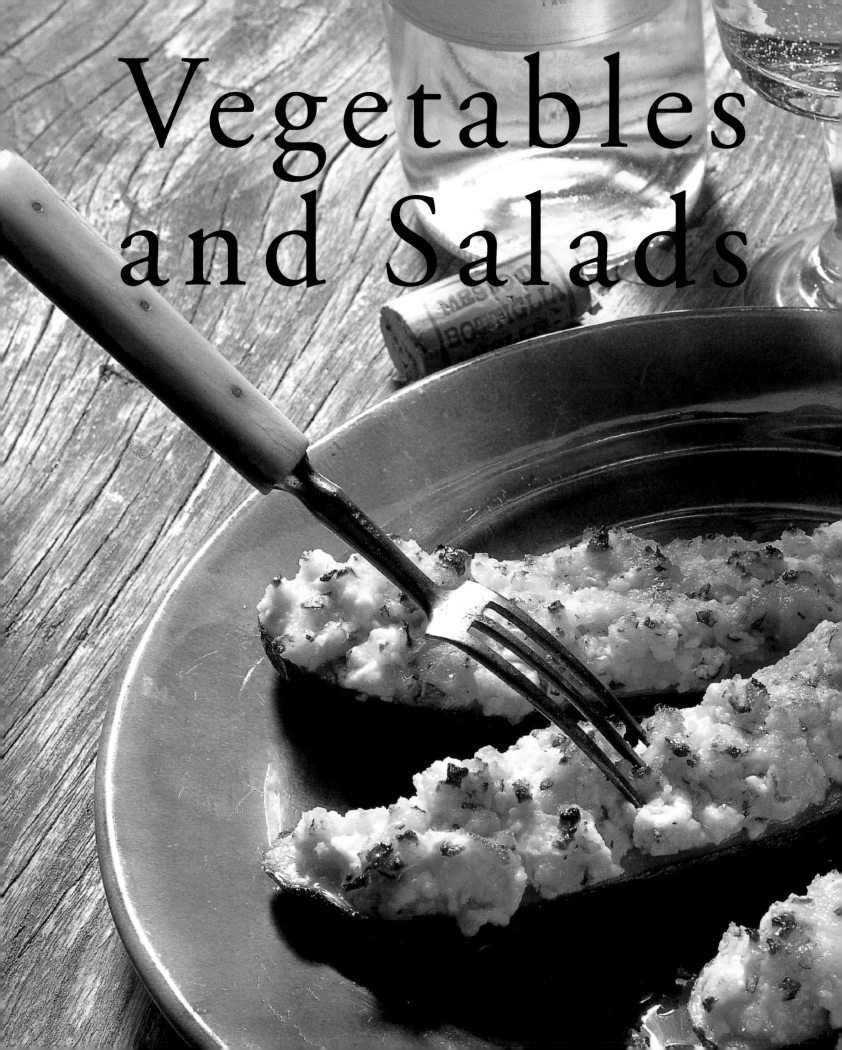

Vegetables and Salads

Mixed Vegetable Salad

A mixture of cooked vegetables makes quite a substantial meal and, as in many Italian dishes, the ingredients may vary according to the vegetables that are available.

3–4 firm tomatoes, sliced

3–4 cups small new potatoes, scraped, boiled and sliced

½ cup boiled or canned chickpeas (garbanzo beans)

1 cup cooked green beans, trimmed, cut in half and cooked

½ cup boiled or canned red kidney beans

4–5 green onions (scallions), sliced

1 tablespoon chopped fresh basil

4–6 tablespoons olive oil

2 tablespoons red or white wine vinegar

salt and freshly ground black pepper

fresh basil, to garnish

arrange the sliced tomatoes around the edge of a shallow salad bowl or a deep plate. Pile the potatoes into one quarter of the dish.

pile the chickpeas (garbanzo beans) next to them, then the green beans, and finally the red kidney beans. If you are using canned chickpeas and kidney beans, drain them well before adding to the salad.

sprinkle the green onions (scallions) around the edge of the dish and the chopped basil over the vegetables, and refrigerate until required.

whisk together the oil and vinegar, and season well with salt and pepper. Just before serving, whisk the oil and vinegar again and pour over the salad.

Serves 4–6
Preparation time: *25–30 minutes*

clipboard: If you wish, a crushed clove of garlic can be added to the oil and vinegar. When cooking the green beans, leave them slightly crisp so they give "bite" to the salad. Remember that dried beans and chickpeas need to be soaked thoroughly before cooking.

Tomato Salad
with anchovies and cumin

The combined flavors of tomato, mustard, anchovies, and cumin make a biting, piquant salad. For a more substantial dish, garnish the salad with slices of hard-boiled egg.

1 heaping tablespoon French mustard
2 tablespoons white or red wine vinegar
6 tablespoons olive oil
4–5 firm tomatoes, sliced
1 stick celery, cut into thin finger-length strips
1 red onion, diced
1 teaspoon cumin seeds
2 anchovy fillets, chopped
salt and pepper
2 hard-boiled eggs to garnish, (optional)

place the mustard in a small bowl and stir in the vinegar. Season lightly with salt and plenty of pepper.

whisk in the olive oil until the mixture is well blended.

place the tomatoes in a salad bowl with the celery, onion, cumin seeds, and anchovy fillets.

pour on the dressing, mix well, garnish with the hard-boiled eggs if using, and serve.

Serves 4
Preparation time: *20 minutes*

clipboard: Red onions are ideal for this salad. They look attractive and have a sweet taste. If they are not available, chopped green onions (scallions) make a good alternative.

Braised Zucchini
with mozzarella and tomatoes

Zucchini have a great affinity with tomato sauce, and this is a way of giving them a robust, hearty flavor.

2 tablespoons oil
2 tablespoons butter
1 shallot, chopped
6 zucchini, cut into 2 inch sticks
1¾ cups canned can plum tomatoes
2 tablespoons Chicken Broth (see page 11)
20 black olives, halved and pitted
¼ teaspoon chopped oregano
1 tablespoon chopped parsley
1 Mozzarella cheese, cubed
salt and pepper

heat the oil and butter in a large, shallow pan, add the chopped shallot, and cook over a low heat until softened.

add the zucchini and cook for a few minutes over a high heat, then reduce the heat to medium.

add the tomatoes, mashed with a fork, season with salt and pepper, and cook until the zucchini are tender, adding a little broth if necessary.

add the halved and pitted olives, oregano, and parsley. Cube the Mozzarella cheese and scatter over the top. Cover the pan, remove from the heat, and leave to stand for a few minutes before serving.

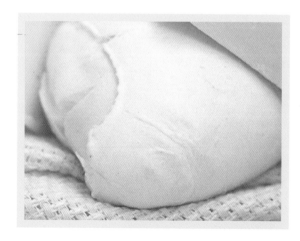

Serves 4
Preparation time: *20 minutes*
Cooking time: *20 minutes*

Cheeses

Dolcelatte

Emmental

Parmesan

Gorgonzola

Gorgonzola

Gorgonzola is a creamy yellow semi-soft cheese with distinctive blue-green veins and a rich, strong flavor. It was first produced over a thousand years ago in Gorgonzola, a village in the north of Italy, and is one of the world's oldest cheeses. It can be used in cooking or eaten by itself and is often served with fresh fruits. If unavailable, use blue cheese.

Emmental

Emmental is a world-famous hard cheese which is pale yellow in color and made from cows' milk. It has a delicately mild, nutty flavor. This Swiss cheese is easily recognized by the large, evenly spaced holes which are distributed throughout the cheese. If unavailable, use other mild-flavored, Swiss-style cheese.

Parmesan

Parmesan is Parma's famous, cow's milk cheese, which is hard and grainy textured. It is pale yellow in color with a strong flavor and aroma. It can be left to mature for up to 3 years. It is sold in a block and is generally grated finely and sprinkled over dishes. It can also be bought grated in a vacuum pack but it is always best to buy it in a block if possible.

Dolcelatte

Dolcelatte is a factory-made cheese, a mass produced version of Gorgonzola. It has the same, characteristic blue veins. Although it doesn't claim the classic status of that great cheese, it is nevertheless very pleasant-tasting. It has a creamy velvet-smooth texture and a mild, sweet taste. If unavailable, use any mild-flavored blue cheese.

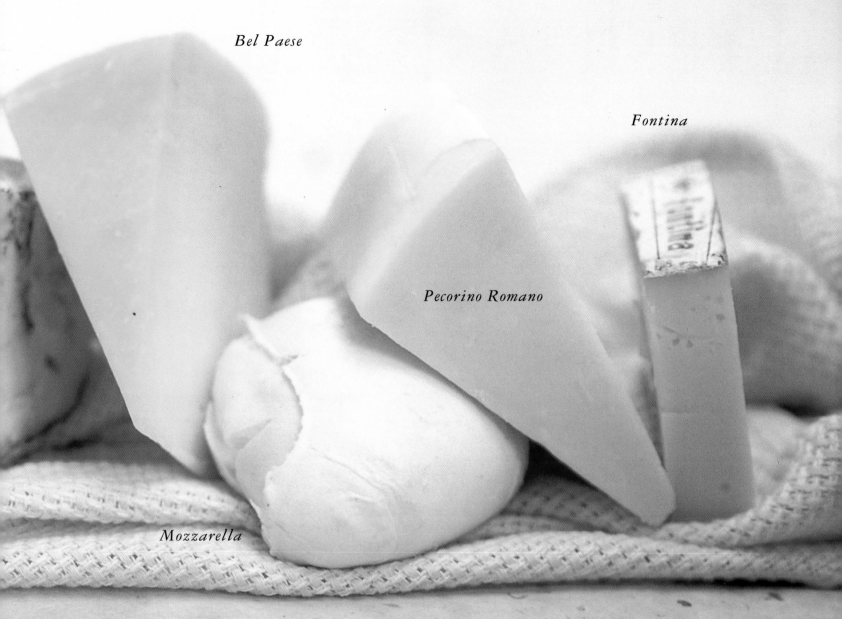

Bel Paese

Fontina

Pecorino Romano

Mozzarella

Bel Paese
Bel Paese is a relatively modern invention, and is one of the world's most popular "easy-eating" cheeses. It is a soft cheese which has a creamy, mild flavor, and a shiny yellow rind. It is made from cow's milk. Bel Paese was first made in the 1920's in Lombardy in Italy, but it is now produced all over Europe. The name means "beautiful country."

Mozzarella
Mozzarella is a white curd cheese with a soft, chewy texture and a mild, milky flavor. It is molded into balls and wrapped in small bags with whey added to keep it moist. Originally it was only made from buffalo's milk, but it is now more often made from cow's milk, or a mixture of both. It is eaten fresh, or used in cooking, for pizza or pasta.

Pecorino Romano
Pecorino Romano is a hard, grating cheese not dissimilar to Parmesan. It has been made for two thousand years in Southern Italy. The main ingredient is sheep's milk, and this gives the cheese a very distinctive salty, tangy taste. The name is taken from the word "pecora" which means ewe. There are several kinds of pecorino, which is used like Parmesan.

Fontina
Genuine Fontina is made exclusively in the Val d'Aosta region of northern Italy. Fontina is reminiscent of Swiss Gruyère, but it is softer and sweeter with much smaller holes. It is a really superb table cheese — soft but sliceable and pale yellow in colour. Fontina is made from cow's milk, and is good for cooking, as well as for eating by itself.

Fresh Asparagus
with tarragon sauce

3 bunches whole asparagus
3 tablespoons tuna in oil
2 anchovy fillets
1 cup olive oil
2 tablespoons white wine
2 tablespoons chopped tarragon
2 hard-boiled eggs
juice of ¼ lemon
salt and white pepper
few sprigs of fresh tarragon, to garnish

trim the ends from the asparagus and scrape or peel away the tough skin. Rinse under cold running water. Divide into bundles and tie with string. Stand in a tall pan containing enough boiling salted water to come two-thirds of the way up, and cover the tips with a loose dome made from aluminum foil. Simmer for 8–18 minutes, depending on the thickness of the asparagus.

meanwhile, prepare the sauce: drain and chop the tuna and anchovies. Put them in a blender or food processor with 2–3 tablespoons of the oil, the wine, and the tarragon.

sieve the hard-boiled egg yolks into a bowl and beat to a paste with a wooden spoon. Add a pinch of salt, then slowly trickle in a few drops of oil. Add more oil once the first few drops have been absorbed. Continue stirring, always in the same direction, until all the oil has been used and the mixture is thick and smooth.

add the mixture to the blender with the lemon juice, season with a pinch of salt if necessary, and a little pepper. Blend briefly to mix the ingredients.

drain the asparagus and cut off the white ends (reserve them for soup or broth). Arrange on a heated serving plate and pour the sauce over it. Sift the hard-boiled egg whites over the asparagus before serving, and garnish with a few sprigs of fresh tarragon.

Serves 4
Preparation time: *15 minutes*
Cooking time: *8–18 minutes*

Peas and Onions

with ham

This is a quick variant on the classic "piselli alla Romana", fresh peas with ham. If you use prosciutto, the dish will taste even better.

8–12 pickling onions
4 tablespoons butter
2 cups fresh shelled or frozen peas
1¼ cups Chicken Broth (see page 12)
2 ounces ham, cut into strips
salt and pepper

blanch the onions in boiling salted water for 4–5 minutes. Drain well. Melt the butter in a pan, add the onions and cook gently until golden.

add the fresh peas if using and ⅔ cup of the broth. Season with salt and pepper. Continue cooking gently for 15–20 minutes until the peas and onions are tender.

add more broth if it is necessary, but allow most of it to boil away by the time the peas are cooked.

if frozen peas are used, add the broth to the onions, and cook until they are nearly tender, then add the peas, and cook for 4–5 minutes.

stir in the ham just before the peas are cooked. Check the seasoning and pour into a serving dish.

Serves 4–6
Preparation time: *10–20 minutes*
Cooking time: *30–35 minutes*

Peperonata

Peppers, tomatoes, onions, and garlic braised in olive oil are the simple ingredients of this colorful Italian classic. It is equally delicious served hot or cold.

⅓ cup olive oil
1⅓ cups finely sliced onions
2 garlic cloves, crushed
6 red and yellow bell peppers, cored, seeded and quartered
6 ripe tomatoes, peeled and chopped or
1 x1¾ cups canned chopped tomatoes
salt and freshly ground black pepper

heat the oil in a heavy-based pan and gently fry the onions and garlic until they are lightly colored.

add the peppers, cover, and cook over a gentle heat for 10–12 minutes.

add the tomatoes and season well with salt and pepper.

cook uncovered, until the peppers are tender and the liquid has reduced to a thick sauce. Check the seasoning and pour into a serving dish. The peperonata can be served hot or cold.

Serves 4
Preparation Time: *20 minutes*
Cooking Time: *40–45 minutes*

clipboard: If canned tomatoes are used, raise the heat toward the end of the cooking time to evaporate the extra liquid. If you prefer, the peppers can be skinned before being cooked.

Stuffed Zucchini
with ricotta and Parmesan

Zucchini are excellent when baked with a savory stuffing, and this recipe is particularly good.

6 zucchini
2 slices crustless white bread
milk for soaking
⅓ cup ricotta or small-curd cottage cheese
¼ teaspoon dried oregano
I garlic clove, crushed
3 tablespoons grated Parmesan cheese
I egg yolk
salt and freshly ground black pepper

trim the ends from the zucchini and cook in a large saucepan of boiling salted water for 5 minutes. Drain well. Soak the bread in a little milk until soft and then squeeze dry.

cut the zucchini in half lengthwise and carefully scoop out the centers using a teaspoon. You should be left with boat-shaped cases which are ready for filling.

chop the zucchini centers finely and place in a bowl. Add the bread, ricotta, or small-curd cottage cheese, oregano, garlic, Parmesan, egg yolk, salt and freshly ground black pepper. Mix thoroughly. The consistency should be fairly soft. If it is too stiff, add a little milk.

arrange the zucchini cases close together in a single layer in a well-oiled shallow baking tray or ovenproof dish. Fill the cases with the cheese mixture and bake in a preheated oven at 375°F for 35–40 minutes until the zucchini are tender and the filling is golden brown. Serve immediately.

Serves 4
Preparation time: *20 minutes*
Cooking time: *40–45 minutes*
Oven temperature: *375°F*

Cannellini Beans

with bacon and sage

This is a farmer-style recipe from the Italian countryside. Cannellini beans are also called white kidney beans. If you cannot find them, use navy or Great Northern beans.

2 cups dried cannellini beans, soaked overnight

1 celery stalk, chopped

2 bay leaves

4 slices bacon, derinded

4 tablespoons bacon fat

3 tablespoons oil

½ onion, chopped

1 tablespoon chopped sage leaves

sprig of rosemary

garlic clove

3 ripe plum tomatoes, skinned (see page 20), chopped and seeded or 1 cup canned tomatoes, drained, seeded and chopped

½ chicken broth cube

2 tablespoons red wine

salt and freshly ground black pepper

put the beans in a large pan with 2 quarts of water, the chopped celery, and the bay leaves. Bring to a boil and simmer for at least 2 hours until tender.

put the bacon in a small pan with enough water to cover and boil for 10 minutes. When cooked, remove the bacon with a slotted spoon and cut into bite-sized pieces.

chop the bacon fat and put in a shallow pan with the oil. Add the chopped onions, herbs, and crushed garlic, and cook over a medium heat until the onion is golden.

add the drained cooked beans, mix together, season with salt and plenty of pepper, and leave for 10 minutes to allow the flavors to mingle.

add the fresh or canned tomatoes to the pan. Then add the boiled bacon, crumble in the broth cube, and stir in the wine. Leave the sauce to thicken a little, then adjust the seasoning and serve hot.

Serves 4
Preparation time: *30 minutes, plus 8 hours soaking*
Cooking time: *3 hours*

Baked Eggplant

with anchovy and pecorino cheese filling

1¼ pounds small round eggplant
½ cup oil
1 onion, minced
4 anchovy fillets, finely chopped
2½ cups plum tomatoes, skinned (see page 20), seeded, and chopped
1 heaping tablespoon capers, finely chopped
6 basil leaves, torn, plus a few extra to garnish
4 tablespoons pecorino cheese, grated
salt and pepper
basil, to garnish

wash and dry the eggplant, then cut off the tops. Slit the flesh from the top into wedge shapes, making cuts just over half-way down the sides with a sharp knife.

sprinkle with salt and leave upside down on an inclined chopping board for 30 minutes to drain off the bitter juices. Rinse well.

heat one-third of the oil in a shallow pan, add the onion, and cook over a medium heat until golden. Add the drained anchovies and cook until they are softened.

stir in the tomatoes, capers, and basil, and season with pepper. Continue cooking this mixture until the sauce has thickened. Remove from the heat and add the pecorino.

dry the eggplant on absorbent paper towel and put them in a baking dish. Open them out a little, fill with the prepared sauce, trickle the remaining oil over the top. Bake in a preheated oven at 350°F for 30 minutes. Serve immediately, garnished with fresh herbs.

Serves: 4
Preparation time: *15 minutes plus draining*
Cooking time: *45 minutes*
Oven temperature: *350°F*

Fresh herbs

Rosemary

Basil

Fennel

Marjoram

Rosemary

Italians adore Rosemary, and use it extensively. It is a perennial herb with long, spiky green leaves and pale blue flowers. When fresh it is very strongly flavored and aromatic. It is often used to flavor vinegars and salads. Italians like using it to flavor lamb and suckling pig. It can be bought fresh or dried and is also very easy to cultivate at home

Basil

Basil is arguably the most important herb used in Italian cooking. Its bright green leaves have a unique flavor, and wonderfully spicy aroma. Basil combines beautifully with tomatoes, which are also essential in Italian cooking. It is the main ingredient in *pesto* a very popular basil sauce often served with pasta. Basil is also frequently used in salads.

Fennel

Fennel is used extensively in Italian cooking. The bulb and the stalks can be eaten either raw or braised. Fennel is often served as a hot vegetable or eaten raw in salads. The bright green, feathery leaves of wild fennel resemble dill, and are chopped up and used to flavor sauces. The seeds are also used in spiced meats.

Marjoram

Marjoram comes from the same family as oregano. It is a herb with small, grey-green leaves and mauve and white flowers. Marjoram is very aromatic, with a sweet, spicy flavor. It is often associated with chicken, pasta dishes, tomatoes, and other vegetable dishes. It should be added at the end of cooking. In Italy it is used as a variant of oregano or combined with it.

Sage

Juniper

Thyme

Bay leaves

Sage

Sage is a gray-green herb with pink and purple flowers, and leaves that have a velvety sheen. It is very aromatic with a slightly bitter taste. It features in Italian veal and calf's liver recipes, also in cheese, and pasta dishes. It is widely available fresh or dried.

Juniper

The berries of the juniper bush are dark, and very similar to peppercorns. Juniper is very aromatic, with a spicy perfume. It is especially good with meat, but should be used sparingly as it can be bitter. Juniper is used in pork and game dishes, and in marinades.

Thyme

Thyme is a small, bushy shrub with gray-green leaves and small pink, purple, red, or white flowers. Thyme has a fragrant aroma and a clove-like taste. Although used less frequently in Italian cooking, it sometimes flavors tomato sauces or marinades, or is included in a _bouquet garni_. It can be bought fresh or dried.

Bay leaves

The leaves of the bay tree are dark green, glossy, and pungent. Because of its strong aroma it is used as an herb. Fully grown bay trees are rare, they are mostly grown as a bushy shrub or small tree in a pot or tub. The leaves are used to flavor soups, casseroles, and pasta dishes. Bay leaves are also an essential ingredient in a _bouquet garni_.

Vegetable Fritatta

Italian omelets are similar in style to the Spanish, with all kinds of ingredients incorporated into the basic mixture. You can happily adapt this to any other vegetable combo that you have available.

3 tablespoons olive oil

2 onions, very finely sliced

3 zucchini, finely sliced

3 tomatoes, skinned (see page 20) and chopped

6 large eggs

4 tablespoons grated Parmesan cheese

few fresh basil leaves, torn

1 tablespoon chopped fresh parsley

2 tablespoons butter

salt and freshly ground black pepper

heat the olive oil in a large, heavy-based skillet. Add the sliced onions and sauté very gently for 8–10 minutes until really soft, golden brown, and almost caramelized. Add the zucchini and continue cooking until golden on both sides, stirring from time to time. Add the tomatoes and cook over moderate heat until the mixture is thick.

break the eggs into a large bowl and add the seasoning, grated Parmesan, torn basil, and parsley. Beat well with a wire whisk until all the ingredients are thoroughly blended.

drain off and discard any excess oil from the cooked tomato mixture. Add the mixture to the beaten eggs and stir together gently until they are well mixed.

heat the butter in a large clean skillet until hot and sizzling. Pour in the egg mixture and reduce the heat to a bare simmer (as low as it will go). Cook very gently until the omelet is firm and set underneath. Place under a preheated hot broiler for a few seconds to set and brown the top. Slide out on to a plate and serve at room temperature cut into wedges.

Serves 4
Preparation time: *25 minutes*
Cooking time: *10–15 minutes*

Baked Eggplant
with cheese and basil

3 pounds eggplant
½ cup olive oil
1 onion, minced
16 tomatoes, skinned (see page 20)
and chopped
3 fresh basil leaves, torn, or 2 teaspoons dried basil
flour for dusting
⅔ cup grated Parmesan cheese
8 ounces Mozzarella cheese, finely sliced
salt and freshly ground black pepper

trim the stems from the eggplant and slice them into rounds. Sprinkle each slice with a little salt and place the salted slices in a colander. Cover the eggplant with a plate and add weights to squeeze out the juices. Leave the eggplant to drain for about 30 minutes.

meanwhile make the tomato sauce. Heat 4 tablespoons of the olive oil in a heavy-based skillet and fry the onion until soft and golden. Add the chopped tomatoes and basil, mix well, and simmer gently, uncovered, until the mixture reduces to a thick sauce. Season to taste with salt and pepper.

rinse the eggplant slices thoroughly in cold water to remove the saltiness. Pat dry with absorbent kitchen paper and dust them with flour. Heat a little of the remaining olive oil in a large skillet and fry the eggplant in batches, adding more oil as needed, until they are cooked and golden brown on both sides. Drain on absorbent kitchen paper.

oil an ovenproof dish and arrange a layer of eggplant slices in the bottom of the dish. Sprinkle with Parmesan and cover with Mozzarella slices. Spoon some of the tomato sauce over the top and continue layering up in this way until all the ingredients have been used, ending with a layer of tomato sauce and Parmesan. Bake in a preheated oven at 400°F for 30 minutes. Serve hot, warm or cold, as preferred.

Serves 4
Preparation time: *40 minutes, plus 30 minutes draining*
Cooking time: *1 hour*
Oven temperature: *400°F*

Spinach Tart
with ricotta and nutmeg

2 cups all-purpose flour
pinch of salt
½ cup butter
I egg yolk
2–3 tablespoons iced water

Filling
2 cups small tender spinach leaves
1½ cups ricotta cheese
4 eggs, beaten
grated nutmeg
⅓ cup light cream
2 tablespoons grated Parmesan cheese
salt and freshly ground black pepper

sift the flour and salt into a mixing bowl and rub in the butter. Mix in the egg yolk and sufficient iced water to make a soft dough. Knead lightly until smooth. Leave in the refrigerator for at least 30 minutes to rest. Roll out the dough to line a 10 inch pie pan.

prick the base of the pastry case with a fork. Line it with a circle of baking paper, and half-fill with ceramic baking beans or ordinary dried beans. Bake in a preheated oven at 400°F for 15 minutes.

remove the baking beans and paper and then return to the oven for a further 5 minutes to cook the base.

make the filling: cook the spinach in a little salted water for 3 minutes until softened but still a fresh bright green color. Drain in a colander and squeeze out any excess water by pressing down hard with a plate. Chop the drained spinach.

put the ricotta in a bowl and beat in the chopped spinach, eggs, nutmeg, salt, and pepper. Beat in the cream and continue beating until smooth. Spoon the filling into the pastry case and smooth the top.

sprinkle with Parmesan and bake at 350°F for 30 minutes until risen, set, and golden brown.

Serves 8
Preparation time: *30 minutes, plus 30 minutes resting*
Cooking time: *30 minutes*
Oven temperatures: *400°F then at 350°F.*

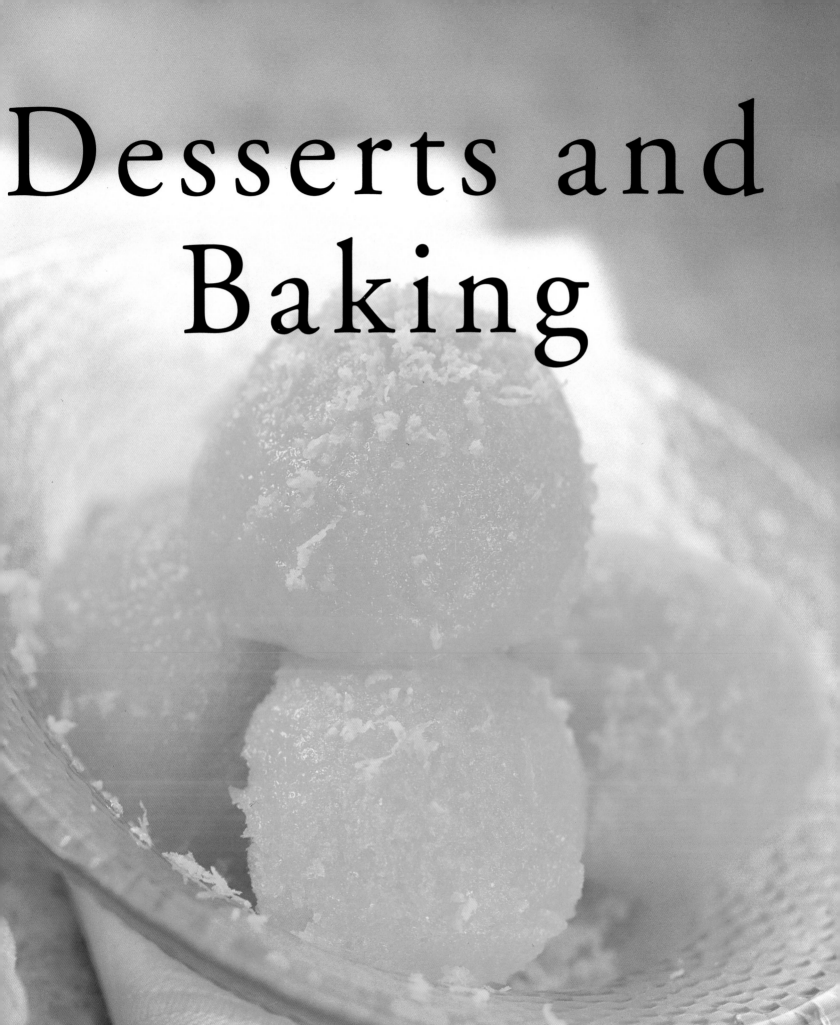

Desserts and Baking

Sicilian Cheesecake

3 eggs, separated
½ cup superfine sugar
finely grated rind of ½ lemon
1 cup all-purpose flour
1 teaspoon baking powder

Filling
¾ cup superfine sugar
3 cups ricotta cheese
⅛ teaspoon ground cinnamon
3¼ cups mixed candied fruits, coarsely chopped
3 ounces baking chocolate, chopped in small pieces
8 tablespoons cherry liqueur
extra cinnamon, to decorate

make the sponge cake: whisk the egg yolks with the sugar, lemon rind, and 3 tablespoons of hot water until light and foaming. Sift the flour and baking powder together and fold it gently into the egg yolk mixture.

whisk the egg whites until they are stiff but not dry. Fold them into the sponge mixture. Pour the mixture into a buttered 10 inch springform pan and bake in a preheated oven at 375°F for 15–20 minutes, or until the cake is golden and springs back when pressed. Unmold and cool.

make the filling: dissolve the sugar in 3 tablespoons of water over low heat. Beat the syrup with the ricotta cheese until well blended. Beat the cinnamon into the ricotta mixture and set aside a few tablespoons for decoration. Stir 1 cup of the chopped candied fruits and chocolate into the rest of the mixture.

line the base of the springform pan with nonstick baking paper. Cut the sponge in half crosswise and put one layer on the base, cut side uppermost. Sprinkle with half of the liqueur and spread with the ricotta mixture. Place the other sponge layer on top and sprinkle with the remaining liqueur. Fit the ring of the pan in position and chill for several hours. To serve, remove from the pan, coat the top and sides with the reserved ricotta mixture, and decorate with the reserved chopped fruit and a sprinkling of cinnamon. .

Serves 6–8
Preparation time: *40 minutes, plus 2–3 hours chilling*
Cooking time: *20–25 minutes*
Oven temperature: *375°F*

Zabaglione

Simple ingredients produce this feather-light, foamy, whipped dessert. Make it immediately before serving, as it is liable to separate if left to stand for more than a few minutes.

4 eggs, separated
5 tablespoons superfine sugar
8 tablespoons Marsala or sweet white wine

To serve
amaretti (almond cookies)

separate the eggs and put the egg yolks in the top of a double boiler or in a bowl sitting over a small saucepan of gently simmering water. Make sure that the bowl is not in contact with the water below.

add the sugar and Marsala or sweet white wine to the egg yolks and mix together thoroughly..

beat the mixture with either a wire whisk or a hand-held electric whisk until the zabaglione is thick, light, and hot. Even with an electric whisk, this will take 10–15 minutes, so be patient. Check that the water simmers gently underneath and does not boil dry.

when the zabaglione is cooked, pour it carefully into 4 tall glasses and serve immediately, with sponge fingers or amaretti. To serve it cold, continue beating the mixture away from the heat until it has cooled completely. The cold zabaglione can be mixed with raspberries, sliced strawberries or peaches.

Serves 4
Preparation time: *2–3 minutes*
Cooking time: *10–15 minutes*

Panettone

Traditionally a Christmas treat, this rich yeast cake from Milan is now eaten throughout the year. At Easter, it is made in the shape of a dove and called Columba.

4 tablespoons superfine sugar

2 tablespoons fresh yeast

⅔ cup lukewarm water

3 egg yolks

pinch of salt

3¾ cups all-purpose flour

½ cup butter, softened

2 tablespoons golden raisins

2 tablespoons raisins

2 tablespoons chopped mixed candied peel

2 tablespoons butter, melted

stir 1 teaspoon of the sugar and all of the yeast into the lukewarm water. Leave to stand for about 10 minutes or until frothy. Beat the egg yolks in a large bowl and stir in the yeast mixture, salt, and remaining sugar. Beat in 2 cups of the flour and then gradually beat in the softened butter, a little at a time. Knead in the remaining flour to make a dough.

turn out the dough on to a lightly floured surface and knead well until the dough is firm and elastic. Place in a lightly oiled plastic bag and leave in a warm place until well risen and doubled in size.

turn out the dough on to a lightly floured surface and knead in the all the raisins and the peel. Continue kneading until the fruits are evenly distributed. Place the dough in a greased 7 inch round cake pan and cover with oiled plastic wrap. Leave in a warm place until the dough rises to the top of the pan.

remove the plastic wrap and brush the top of the dough with some of the melted butter. Bake in a preheated oven at 400°F for 20 minutes. Reduce the oven temperature to 350°F and cook for a further 20–30 minutes. Remove from the pan and brush the top and sides with the remaining melted butter. Serve warm or cold, cut into thin slices.

Serves 10
Preparation time: *1½ hours*
Cooking time: *40–50 minutes*
Oven temperatures: *400°F then 350°F*

Neapolitan Tart
with ricotta and almonds

*The filling in this traditional latticed tart is
rich and fruity, with a distinctive almond flavor.*

2 cups all-purpose flour
pinch of salt
½ cup butter
I egg yolk
2–3 tablespoons iced water
powdered sugar for dusting

Filling
I½ cups ricotta cheese
3 tablespoons superfine sugar
3 eggs, well beaten
4 tablespoons blanched almonds, finely chopped
2 tablespoons chopped mixed peel
finely grated rind of ½ lemon
juice and finely grated rind of ½ orange
¼ teaspoon vanilla extract

sift the flour and salt into a mixing bowl and rub in the butter with the fingertips until the mixture resembles fine bread crumbs. Mix in the egg yolk and add enough iced water to form a soft dough. Knead lightly and leave to chill in the refrigerator for 30 minutes. Roll out the dough to line an 8 inch pie pan. Reserve the dough trimmings.

make the filling: rub the ricotta cheese through a sieve into a basin and then beat in the sugar. Gradually beat in the eggs and then add the almonds, peel, lemon and orange rind and juice, and the vanilla extract, beating well between each addition.

pour the ricotta cheese filling into the prepared pastry case and then smooth the surface.

roll out the reserved dough trimmings then, using a fluted pastry wheel, cut into long ½ inch wide strips. Arrange them in a latticework pattern over the top of the flan. Bake in the center of a preheated oven at 350°F for 45–50 minutes or until set and golden. Cool and serve cold, but not chilled, dusted with powdered sugar.

Serves 6–8
Preparation time: *20 minutes, plus 30 minutes chilling*
Cooking time: *45–50 minutes*
Oven temperature: *350°F*

Caramelized Oranges

If you have plenty of oranges, and want to make a really pretty, fresh-tasting dessert, this is a simple and quickly made recipe.

12 oranges
¾ cup sugar
½ cup water

pare the rind thinly from one of the oranges and cut it into thin strips. Cook the strips in a small pan of boiling water for 2–3 minutes or until softened. Drain well and put aside.

remove and discard all the white parts and rind from the oranges with a sharp knife. Put the oranges in a large heatproof bowl. Sprinkle the strips of cooked orange rind over the top.

put the sugar and water in a saucepan and heat gently, stirring constantly, until the sugar dissolves completely. Bring to the boil and boil hard until the syrup changes to a rich golden caramel color. Take care that the caramel does not become too dark; it will continue to cook after the pan is removed from the heat. If it is too thick, stand well back and add 2 tablespoons of hot water, then stir well.

pour the caramel over the oranges and set aside to cool. Place in the refrigerator and leave to chill overnight. To serve, transfer the oranges and caramel to an attractive serving dish and serve with whipped cream. Note: if wished, the oranges can be cut into thin slices horizontally, and secured with toothpicks before adding the caramel.

Serves 6
Preparation time: *15 minutes*
Cooking time: *8–10 minutes, plus chilling time*

Amaretto Soufflés
with almonds and vanilla

4 almond cookies
6 tablespoons Amaretto di Saronno liqueur
⅔ cup milk
1 drop vanilla extract
1 tablespoon butter
2 tablespoons all-purpose flour
4 egg yolks (1 reserved)
4 egg whites
1 tablespoon superfine sugar
sifted powdered sugar to decorate

Almond paste
6 tablespoons flaked almonds
⅔ cup milk
2 teaspoons sugar

make the almond paste: put the almonds, milk, and sugar in a saucepan and bring to a boil.

reduce the heat and simmer gently for a few minutes. Cool slightly and then combine in a food processor or blender until thoroughly blended.

grease and flour 4 individual soufflé dishes, each 3 inches in diameter. Cut the cookies into quarters, then soak them in half the Amaretto and put 1 cookie (four quarters) in each prepared soufflé dish.

make the soufflé mixture: put two-thirds of the milk in a heavy-based saucepan with the vanilla and butter, and bring to a boil. Remove from the heat and stir in the remaining milk with the flour and the one reserved egg yolk.

heat again until the mixture thickens and whisk briefly. Add the remaining egg yolks and cook for 2 minutes over low heat.

whisk the egg whites until stiff and then whisk in the sugar. Blend the soufflé mixture with the almond paste and the remaining Amaretto.

fold in the beaten egg whites carefully. Spoon this mixture into the soufflé dishes and cook in a preheated oven at 425°F for 10–12 minutes. Dust with confectioner's sugar.

Serves 4
Preparation time: *25 minutes*
Cooking time: *15–20 minutes*
Oven temperature:*425°F*

Sicilian Peach Water Ice

Sicilian fruit-based water ices taste wonderful. You can make them with other fruits such as melon, with excellent results.

½ cup sugar
⅔ cup water
4 large peaches or melon (see clipboard below)
juice of 1 lemon

put the sugar and water into a small pan and heat gently until the sugar has dissolved, then boil for 3–4 minutes. Leave until completely cold.

immerse the peaches in boiling water for 1 minute, then drain and remove the skins and pits. Immediately purée the flesh in an electric blender or press through a nylon sieve.

mix with the lemon juice to prevent discoloration. Stir the cold syrup into the mixture, pour into a shallow freezer tray, and freeze until half-frozen.

unmold into a bowl and whisk vigorously for a few minutes, then return to the tray and freeze until firm.

transfer to the refrigerator 30–40 minutes before serving, to allow the ice to thaw a little. To serve, scoop the water ice into individual glasses.

Serves 4
Preparation time: *15 minutes, plus freezing and 30–40 minutes chilling*

clipboard: Melon water ice can be made the same way by replacing the peaches in this recipe with 1½ pounds ripe, peeled and seeded Honeydew or Crenshaw melon flesh.

Almond Peaches
with amaretti filling

*These almond-flavored baked peaches are a speciality
of the Piedmont region in the north of Italy.*

4 large firm peaches, halved and pitted

6 amaretti cookies, crushed (see clipboard below)

2 tablespoons superfine sugar

3 tablespoons butter, softened

1 egg yolk

½ teaspoon finely grated lemon rind

scoop a little flesh from the center of each peach half and put in a bowl.

add the amaretti crumbs, sugar, 2 tablespoons of the butter, the egg yolk, and lemon rind, and beat until smooth.

divide between the peaches, shaping the stuffing into a mound. Top with flaked almonds if desired, and dot with the remaining butter.

arrange in a buttered ovenproof dish. Bake in a preheated moderate oven at 350°F for 25–35 minutes. Serve warm or cold with light cream.

Serves 4
Preparation time: *20 minutes*
Cooking time: *25–35 minutes*
Oven temperature: *350°F*

Clipboard: Amaretti biscuits are very popular in Italy. They have a distinctive almond flavor, and are typical accompaniments to Italian desserts. They are now widely available in large supermarkets, as well as in Italian food shops.

Ricotta Bombe
with rum

Ricotta, a soft, moist, white cheese with a slightly grainy texture, features in a multitude of Italian recipes. Here it is used to make a creamy, ice-cold dessert, a speciality of the countryside around Rome.

5 egg yolks
½ cup superfine sugar
5 tablespoons rum
1 pound fresh ricotta cheese, sifted

line a 1.2-quart freezerproof mold with aluminum foil.

put the egg yolks and sugar in a bowl, and whisk with an electric or hand whisk until light and fluffy.

fold in the rum until it is thoroughly amalgamated, then fold in the ricotta a little at a time.

spoon the mixture into the prepared mold, smooth the surface, then cover with aluminum foil.

freeze until solid. Unmold on to a serving platter and serve immediately with Amaretti or spiced cookies.

Serves 4–6
Preparation time: *20 minutes, plus freezing*

Tiramisù
Mascarpone Coffee Dessert

Mascarpone cheese is a double – or even treble – cream cheese, and Tiramisù is one of the most popular desserts in which it features. If you like, you can decorate the top with grated chocolate.

2 egg yolks

2 tablespoons superfine sugar

few drops vanilla extract

1 cup mascarpone cheese

¾ cup strong black coffee

2 tablespoons Marsala

1 tablespoon brandy

10 lady finger cookies

1 tablespoon cocoa powder

2 tablespoons grated dark chocolate (optional)

mix together the egg yolks and sugar in a bowl, beating with a wooden spoon until they are creamy. Add the vanilla extract and fold in the mascarpone. The mixture should be thick and creamy.

make the strong black coffee in a jug or cafetière, then mix with the Marsala and brandy in a bowl. Quickly dip the lady fingers in the coffee mixture. They should absorb just enough liquid to flavor them without becoming soggy and falling apart.

arrange some of the soaked lady fingers in the base of a large attractive glass serving bowl or 4 individual serving dishes. Cover with a layer of the mascarpone mixture.

continue layering alternate layers of lady fingers and mascarpone, finishing with a top layer of mascarpone. Sift the cocoa powder over the top, then chill in the refrigerator for 3–4 hours or until set. The flavor improves if the coffee dessert is left overnight.

Serves 6
Preparation time: *20 minutes, plus 3–4 hours chilling*

Breads

Pandoro

Panini

Grissini

Panettone

Baguette

Pandoro
Pandoro is a tall, shaped yeast cake which is very similar to panettone but is made without the fruit. It is served for breakfast with coffee and also on special occasions such as Christmas and Easter.

Panini
Panini simply means "little bread" and is a typical Italian table bread, baked in the form of a small, flat, loaf. Like all Italian bread, panini is made with yeast. It is made fresh every day, and served with all meals.

Baguette
The baguette is traditionally associated with France. Originally from Paris, it is a long, thin crusty loaf made with white flour, and it is delicious eaten with cheese. It is an international bread, baked all over the world.

Panettone
Panettone is a yeast cake made with egg yolk and candied fruits. Made in the shape of a tall loaf, it is a speciality of Northern Italy. It is very popular in Europe, and is served for breakfast and special occasions.

Focaccia

Ciabatta

Grissini
Every Italian restaurant worth its salt has welcoming stacks of delicious, crunchy Grissini on the table. It is a long, thin, crisp dry bread which is pale gold in color and is served as an appetizer.

Focaccia
Foccacia is a flat, Italian yeast bread, made with olive oil as a key ingredient and baked in an oiled pan. It is often flavored with garlic. Focaccia is served with different toppings such as sun-dried tomatoes, olives, or fresh herbs. It is equally delicious eaten by itself or with a filling.

Ciabatta
Ciabatta is one of the most popular of all Italian breads. Like foccacia it is made with olive oil, and baked into a fairly flat loaf with a distinctive open texture. Ciabatta can be cooked with a delicious range of flavorings such as sun-dried tomatoes, olives, and herbs.

Garlic Focaccia

Panne all'olio, Italian olive oil bread has become universally popular. It is healthy and delicious, and not at all difficult to make — try this garlic-flavored version.

1 package dry yeast
1 teaspoon sugar
3 cups all-purpose flour
¾ cup lukewarm water
1 teaspoon salt
3 cloves garlic, crushed
2 tablespoons olive oil
1 tablespoon yellow cornmeal or farina
1 tablespoon olive oil, plus extra for glazing
2 teaspoons finely crushed sea salt

combine the yeast, sugar, 1 teaspoon flour, and water in a small mixing bowl. Leave in a warm place, covered with plastic wrap, for 10 minutes or until foaming.

sift the remaining flour and salt into a large mixing bowl. Add the garlic and stir with a knife to combine. Make a well in the center, stir in the yeast mixture and olive oil. Using a flat-bladed knife, mix to a firm dough.

unmold the dough onto lightly floured surface, and knead for 10 minutes. Shape the dough into a ball, and place in a large, lightly oiled mixing bowl. Cover with plastic wrap and stand in a warm place for 40 minutes or until well risen.

preheat the oven to moderately hot, about 425°F. Sprinkle the base of a 7 x 11 inch shallow baking pan with cornmeal or farina. Knead the dough again for 2 minutes or until smooth. Press the dough into the pan and prick deep holes with a skewer.

sprinkle lightly with water and place in the oven. Bake for 10 minutes and sprinkle again with water. Bake for an additional 10 minutes, brush with extra olive oil, sprinkle with sea salt, then bake for 5 more minutes. Serve warm or at room temperature, cut into squares.

Serves 4–6
Preparation time: *20 minutes, plus 50 minutes standing*
Cooking time: *25 minutes*
Oven temperature: *425°F*

Cheese Focaccia
with fresh chives

Cheese and chives complement each other well, and give a robust flavor to the focaccia.

1 package dry yeast
1 teaspoon sugar
3 cups all-purpose flour
¾ cup lukewarm water
1 teaspoon salt
2 tablespoons finely grated Parmesan cheese
1 tablespoon finely chopped chives
2 tablespoons olive oil
1 tablespoon cornmeal or farina
1 tablespoon olive oil plus
extra for glazing
2 teaspoons finely crushed sea salt or kosher salt

combine the yeast, sugar, 1 teaspoon flour, and water in small mixing bowl. Cover with plastic wrap and stand in a warm place for 10 minutes or until foaming.

sift the remaining flour and salt into a large mixing bowl. Add Parmesan and chives, and stir with a knife to combine. Make a well in the center, stir in the yeast mixture and olive oil. Mix to a firm dough with a knife.

unmold the dough onto a lightly floured surface, and knead for 10 minutes. Shape the dough into a ball, and place in a large, lightly oiled mixing bowl. Cover with plastic wrap and stand in a warm place for 40 minutes or until well risen.

preheat oven to moderately hot, 425°F. Sprinkle the base of a 7 x 11 inch shallow pan with cornmeal or farina. Knead the dough again for 2 minutes or until smooth. Press dough into the pan; prick deep holes with a skewer. Sprinkle lightly with water and place in the oven. Bake for 10 minutes and sprinkle again with water. Bake for an additional 10 minutes, brush with the extra olive oil, sprinkle with sea salt, then bake for 5 more minutes. Serve warm or at room temperature, cut into squares.

Serves 4–6
Preparation time: *20 minutes, plus 50 minutes standing*
Cooking time: *25 minutes*
Oven temperature: *425°F*

Olive Focaccia
with rosemary and garlic

1 package dry yeast
1 teaspoon sugar
3 cups all-purpose flour
¾ cup lukewarm water
1 teaspoon salt
1 clove garlic, crushed
2 tablespoons olive oil
¼ - ⅓ cup pitted black olives, finely chopped
1 tablespoon fresh rosemary leaves
1 tablespoon cornmeal or farina
1 tablespoon olive oil, plus extra for glazing
2 teaspoons finely crushed sea salt or kosher salt

To garnish
few whole black olives
few sprigs fresh rosemary

combine the yeast, sugar, 1 teaspoon flour, and water in a small mixing bowl. Cover with plastic wrap and stand in a warm place for 10 minutes or until foaming.

sift the remaining flour and salt into a large mixing bowl. Add the garlic, olives, and rosemary and stir with a knife to combine. Make a well in the center, stir in the yeast mixture and olive oil. Using a flat-bladed knife, mix to a firm dough.

unmold the dough onto a lightly floured surface, and knead for 10 minutes. Shape the dough into a ball, and place in a large, lightly oiled mixing bowl. Cover with plastic wrap and stand in a warm place for 40 minutes or until well risen.

preheat oven to moderately hot, 425°F. Sprinkle the base of a 7 x 11 inch shallow baking pan with cornmeal or farina. Knead the dough again for 2 minutes or until smooth. Press dough into the pan, and prick deep holes with a skewer.

sprinkle lightly with water and place in the oven. Bake for 10 minutes and sprinkle again with water. Bake for an additional 10 minutes, brush with extra olive oil, sprinkle with sea salt, then bake for 5 more minutes. Serve warm or at room temperature, cut into squares.

Serves: 4–6
Preparation time: *15 minutes*
Cooking time: *45 minutes*
Oven temperature: *425°F*

Index

Acknowledgments

Photo Credits
Peter Myers: front jacket
Jean Cazals: back jacket, front flap, back flap

Special photography by Jean Cazals

All other photos:
Octopus Publishing Group Ltd. / William Adams-Lingwood,
Robert Golden, Tim Imrie, Graham Kirk, James Murphy,
Peter Myers, Simon Smith, Roger Stowell, Paul Webster,
Paul Williams.

Home economist
Marie-Ange Lapierre